TURIN DIARY

Peter Bialobrzeski

February 10 – February 16, 2020

Hartmann books

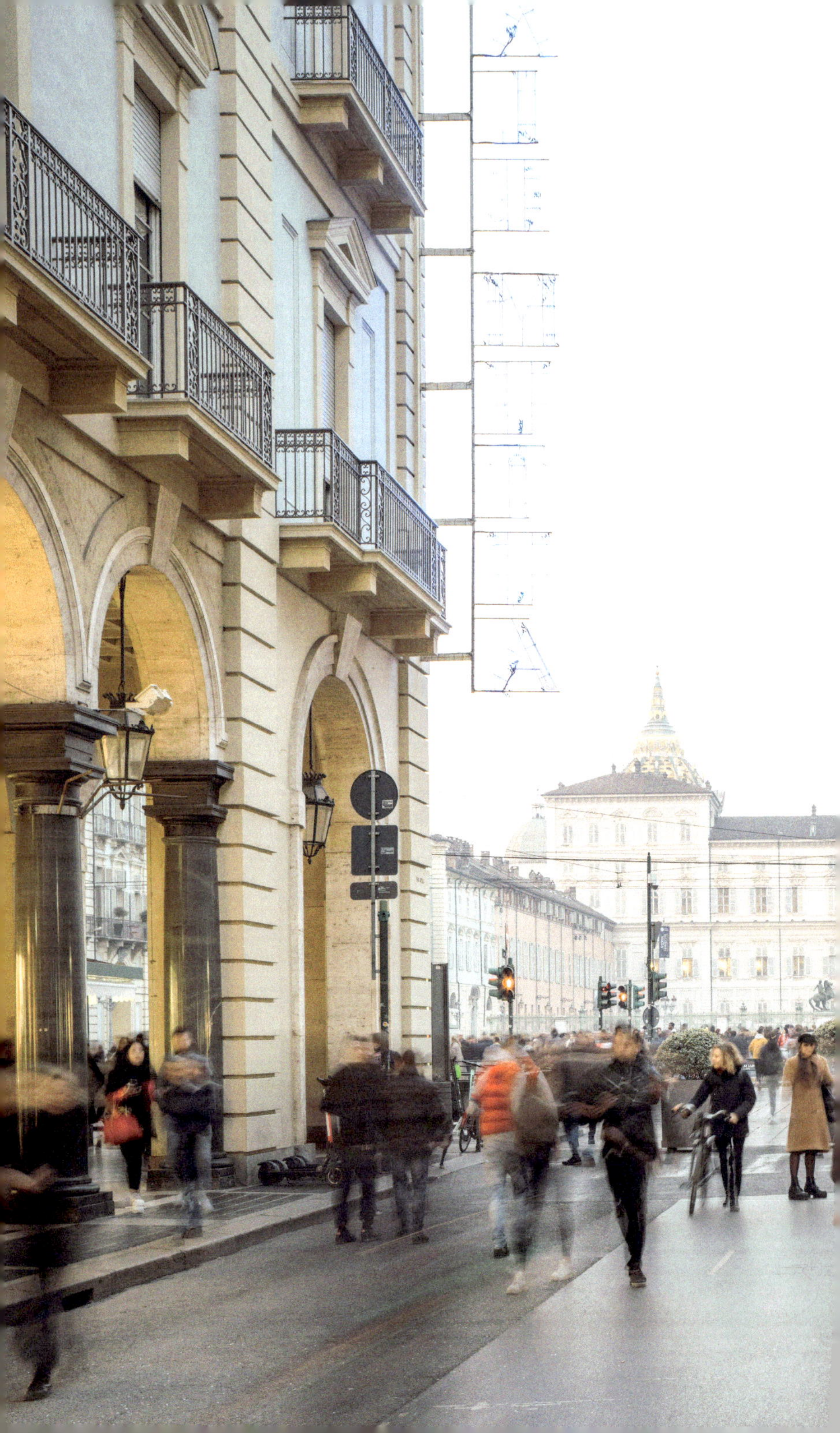

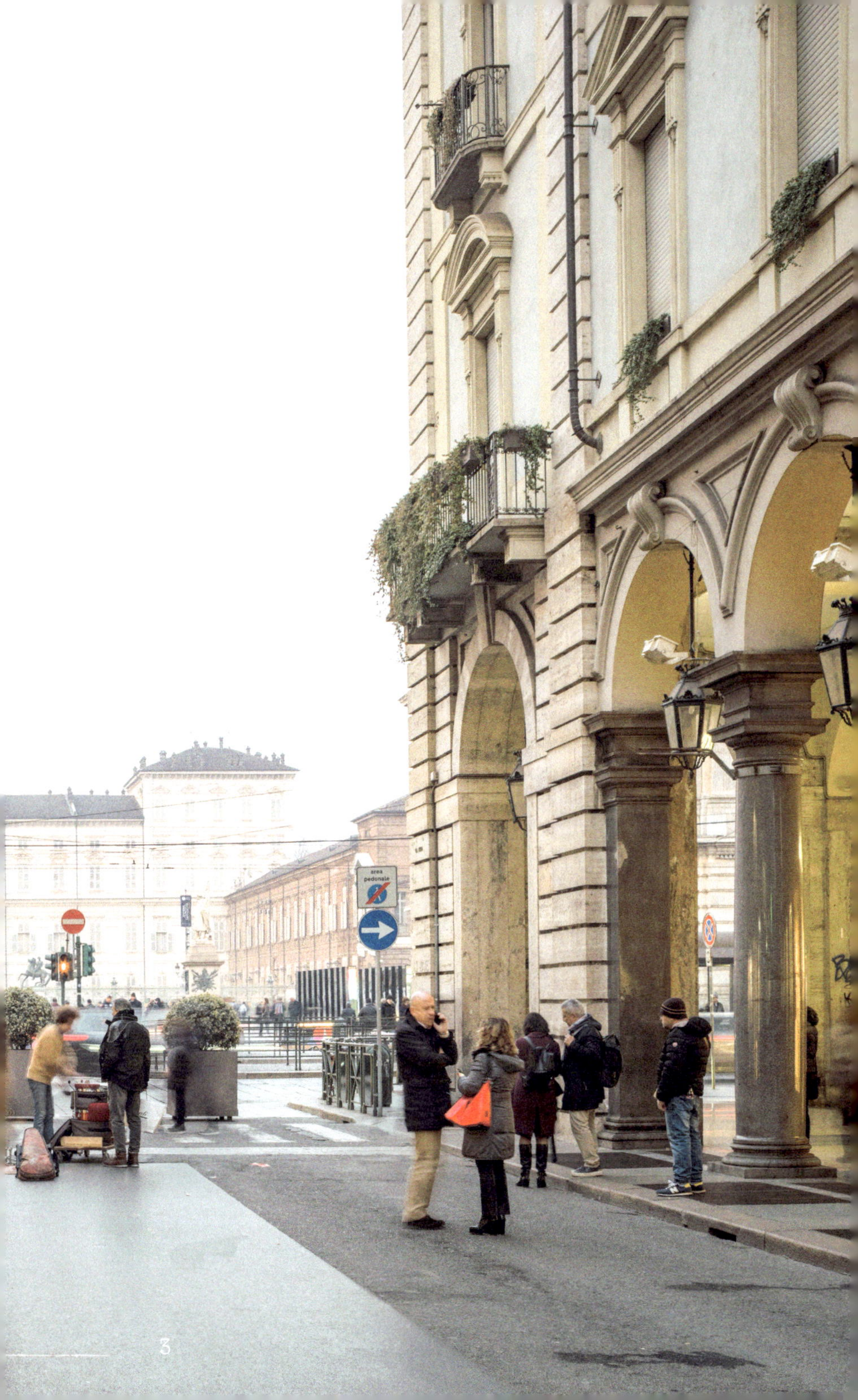
area
pedonale

TURIN DIARY
Peter Bialobrzeski

→ February 10, 2020 After a ten-hour delay due to Hurricane *Sabine*, I finally arrive in the old town of Turin. The weatherman on the radio this morning claimed that this storm was not the result of climate change, but quite normal for this time of year. Whatever: the air already smells and feels like spring, even though it is still chilly. The city of *Fiat*, *Lancia*, *Alfa Romeo*, and *Juventus Turin* welcomes this German visitor with an Italian dinner and a cold beer.
→ February 11, 2020 At the end of the road, beyond the railwaystation, the Alps are visible. A homeless person still sleeps under the city's famous arcades as the traffic comes to life and the old-fashioned neon signs of hotels and bars are turned off in the soft morning light of Piedmont.

→ February 12, 2020 Meanwhile, the former minister of the interior told the Turin newspaper *La Stampa*, "It's crazy, I don't know how much it costs in terms of personnel and money to prove that I'm a criminal, but I'm not afraid and I'll explain that I was defending my country." Matteo Salvini is referring to today's vote in the Senate on whether he should be put on trial for kidnapping 131 migrants last year. He forced them to stay on board a coast guard ship and did not let them disembark to safety. → February 13, 2020 Even though Turin has a number of stunning sights such as the UNESCO World Heritage *Residenze Reali* and the former synagogue that now houses the Cinema Museum, there is a delightful lack of tourists in this pleasant city. According to my friends, rents are low, and I am surprised by the number of tiny outlets that still stock household goods, stationery, and, of course, local delicacies. → February 14, 2020 Salvini came to town yesterday and delivered a speech to a crowd of two hundred supporters. I bumped into them in front of the old *Fiat* factory building, which now serves as a shopping mall, conference center and a hotel. The frightening thing was that among the crowd of the usual suspects, the bald-headed alcoholics whose Facebook feeds one does not want to see, there were a number of welldressed, good-looking bourgeois women. The far right is back—and not just in my home country.→ February 15, 2020 Prog rock with my cappuccino: Pink Floyd's "Welcome to the Machine," a forty-year-old critical homage to the machine age, fits strangely well into the cozy setting of the café. It is followed by "Rikki Don't Lose That Number." Steely Dan. And yes, the city feels like a trip back to the eighties. Dozens of small shops sell everything from men's razing gear to women's lingerie, from light bulbs to old-fashioned children's toys. → February 16, 2020 *Posto Fumo,* a place to smoke, reads a sign on a street that looks as if it were straight out of old Paris. The area behind the *Porta Palazzo*, a huge market , is populated at night by migrants from Asia, Africa, and the Middle East. Today, on this hazy Sunday morning, no one is walking the streets, while just two hundred kilometers to the northeast people, are dying from a mysterious virus.

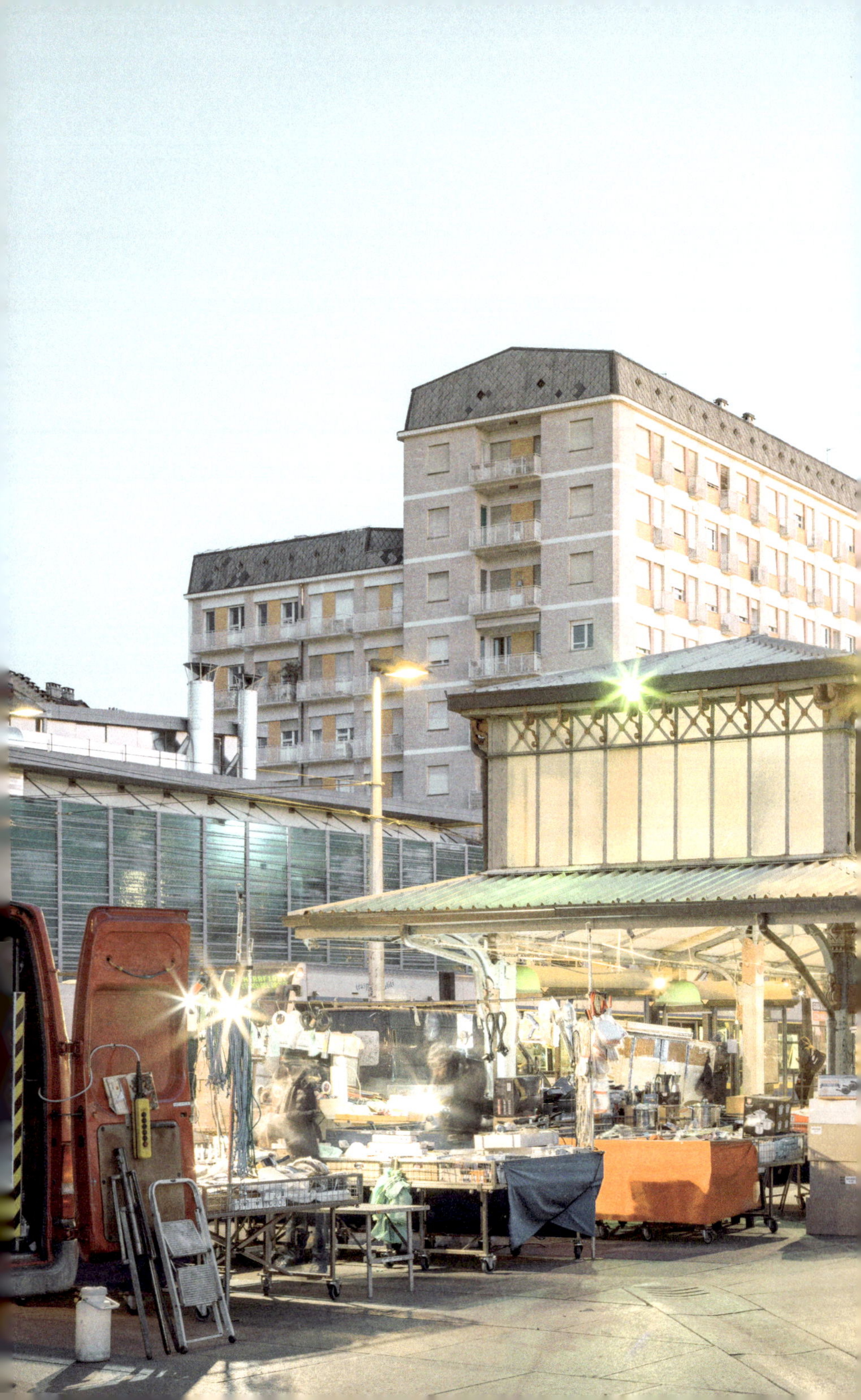

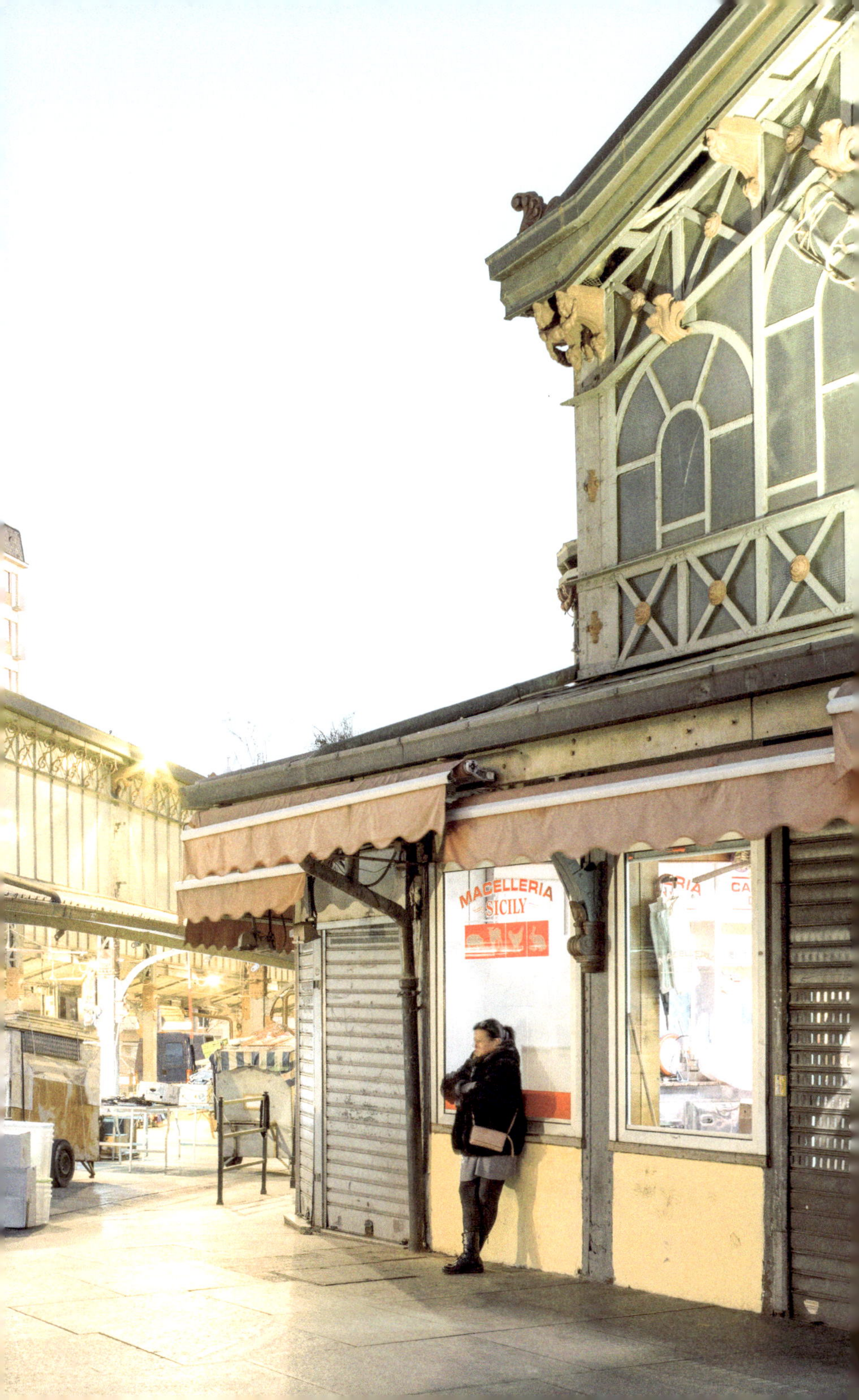
MACELLERIA
SICILY

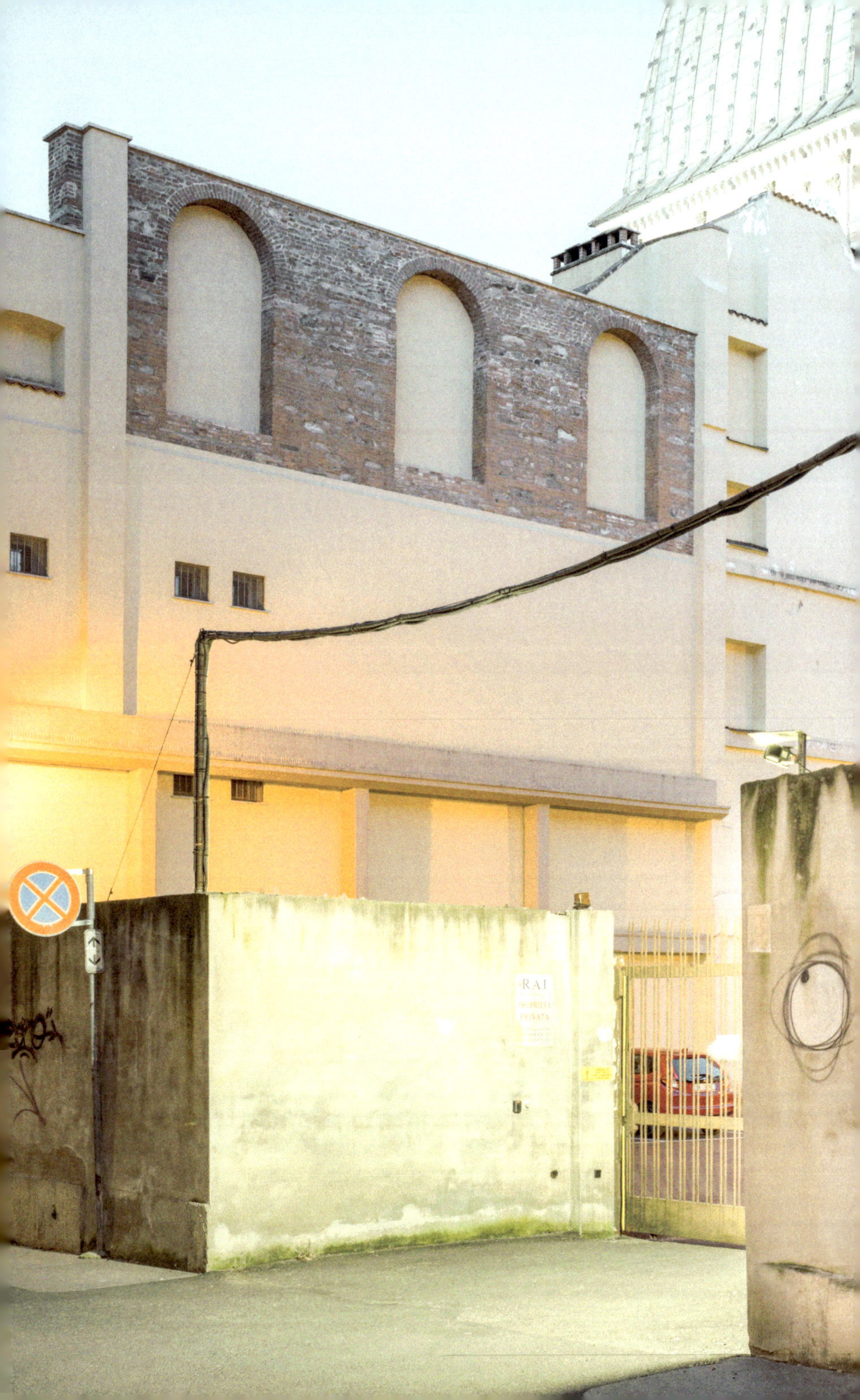
RAI
PRIVATA

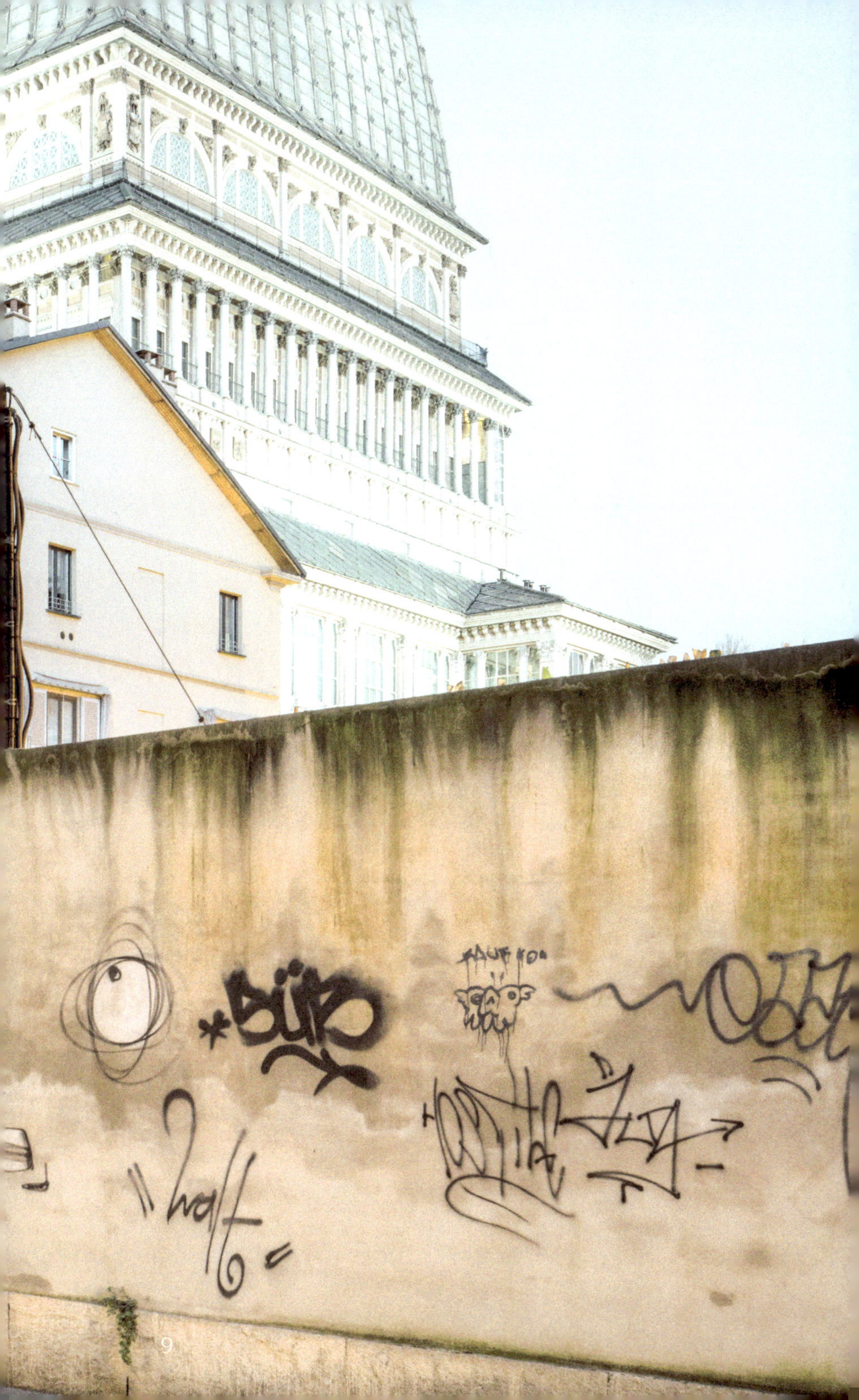

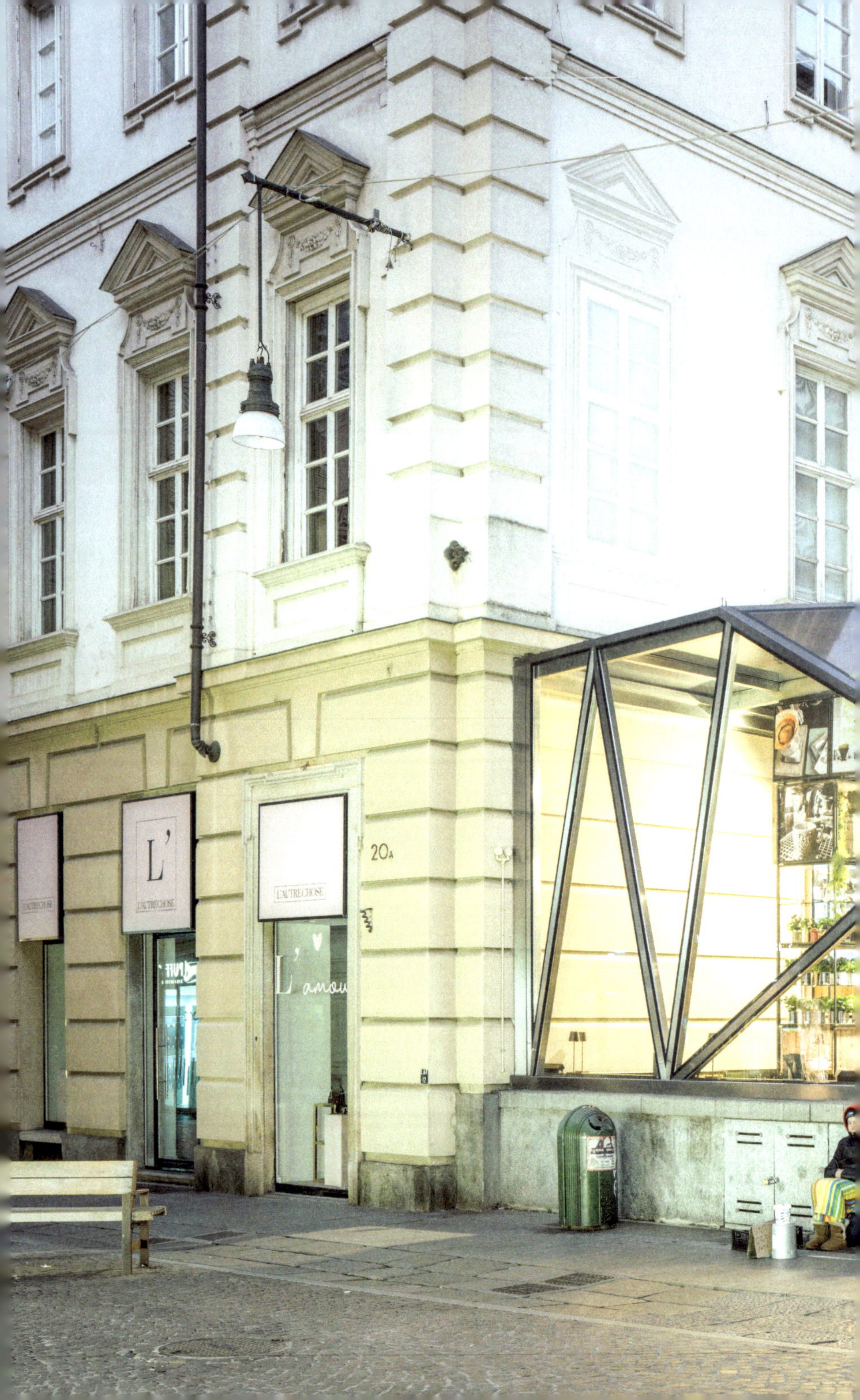

L'
L'AUTRECHOSE
L'AUTRECHOSE
20A

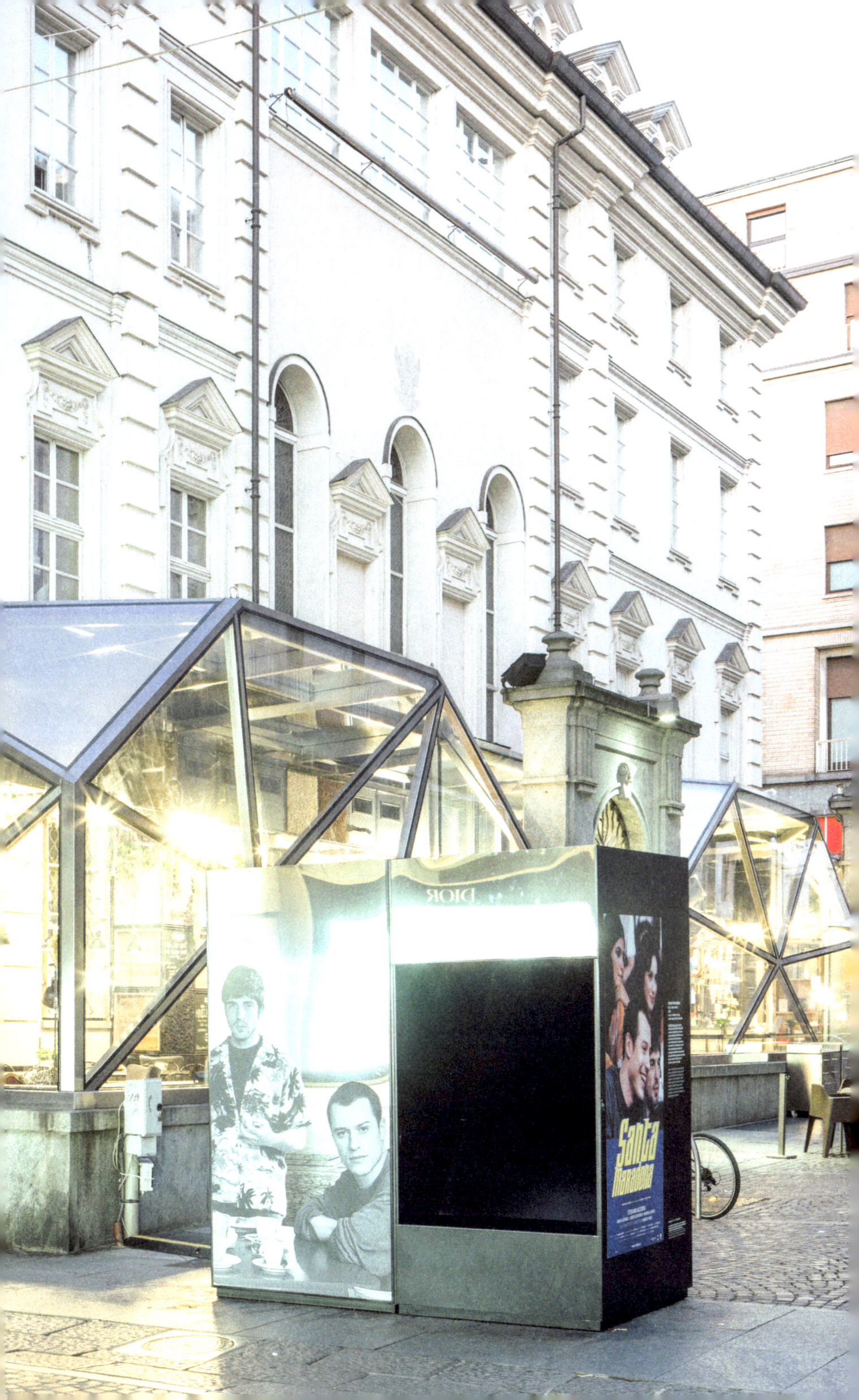
Santa Maradona

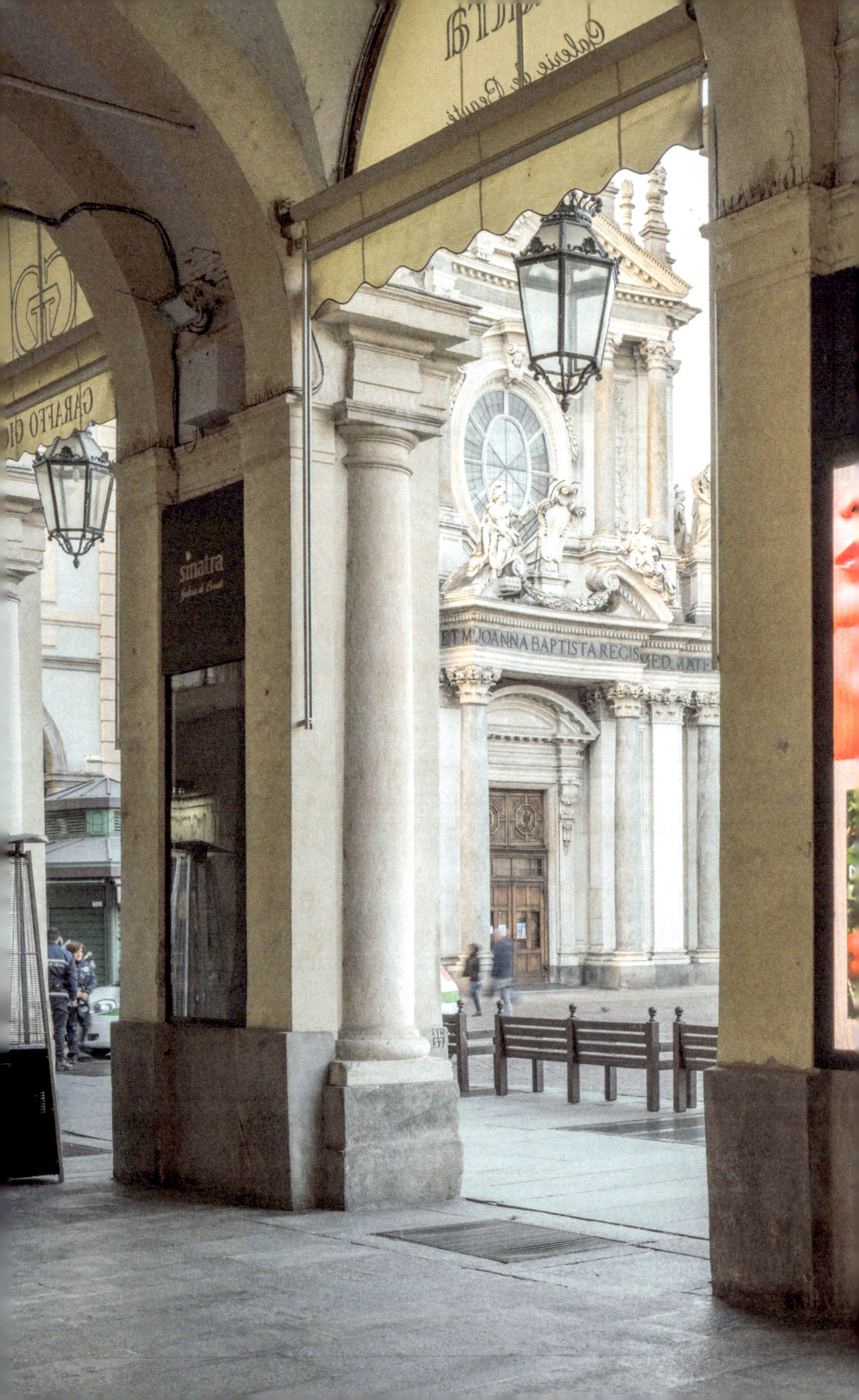
sinatra
ET M. JOANNA BAPTISTA REGIS

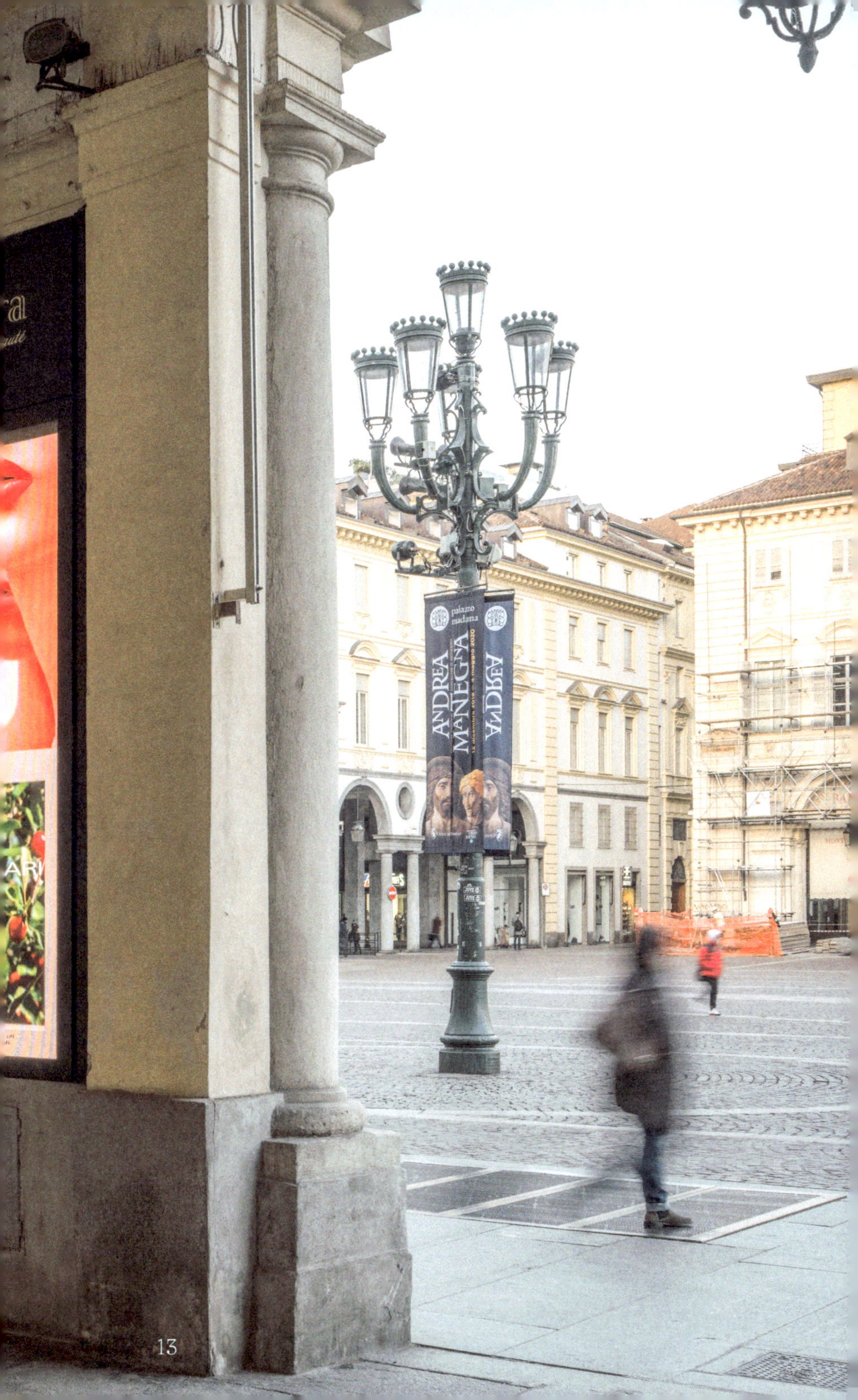
palazzo madama
ANDREA MANTEGNA
12 dicembre 2019 – 4 maggio 2020

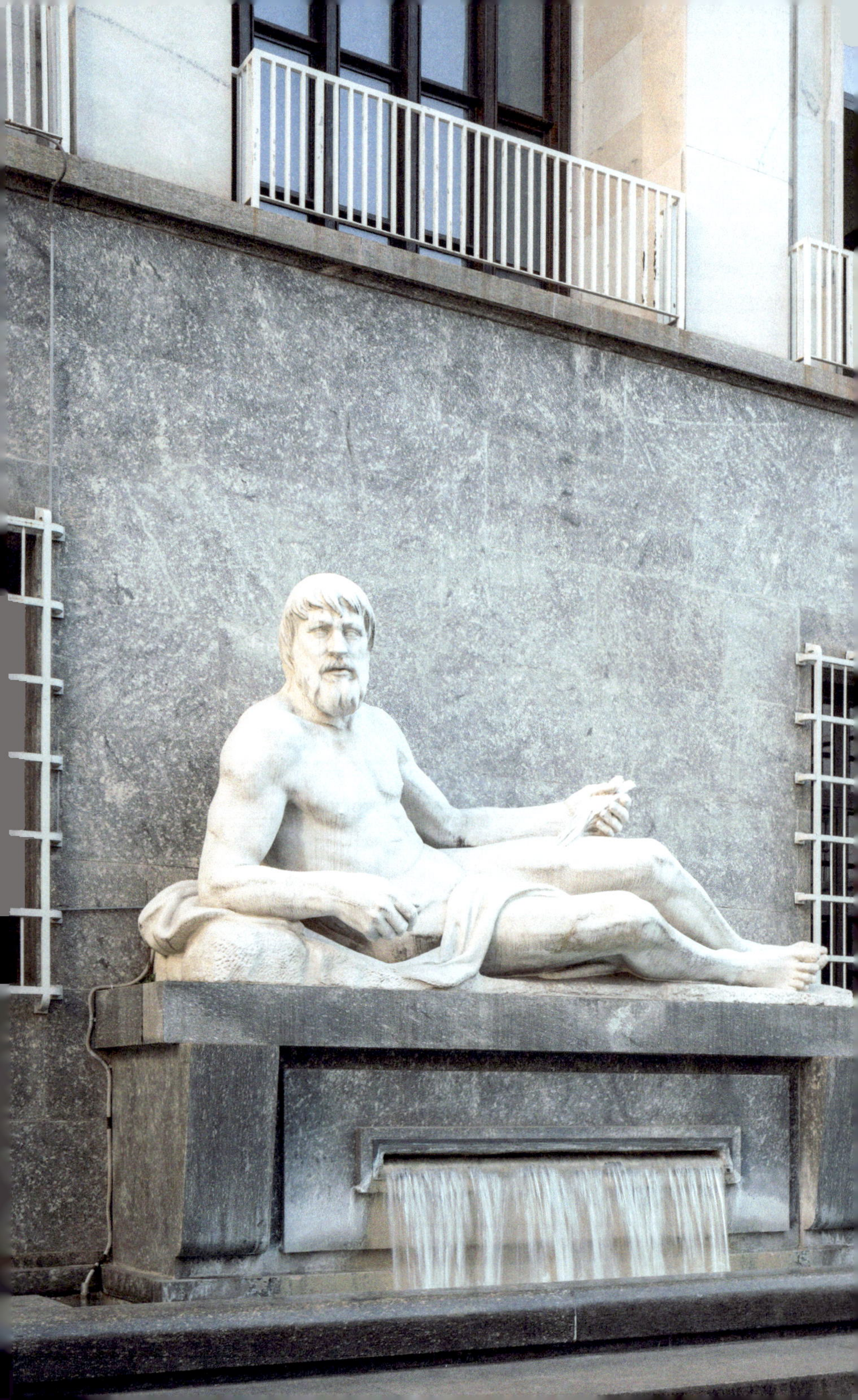

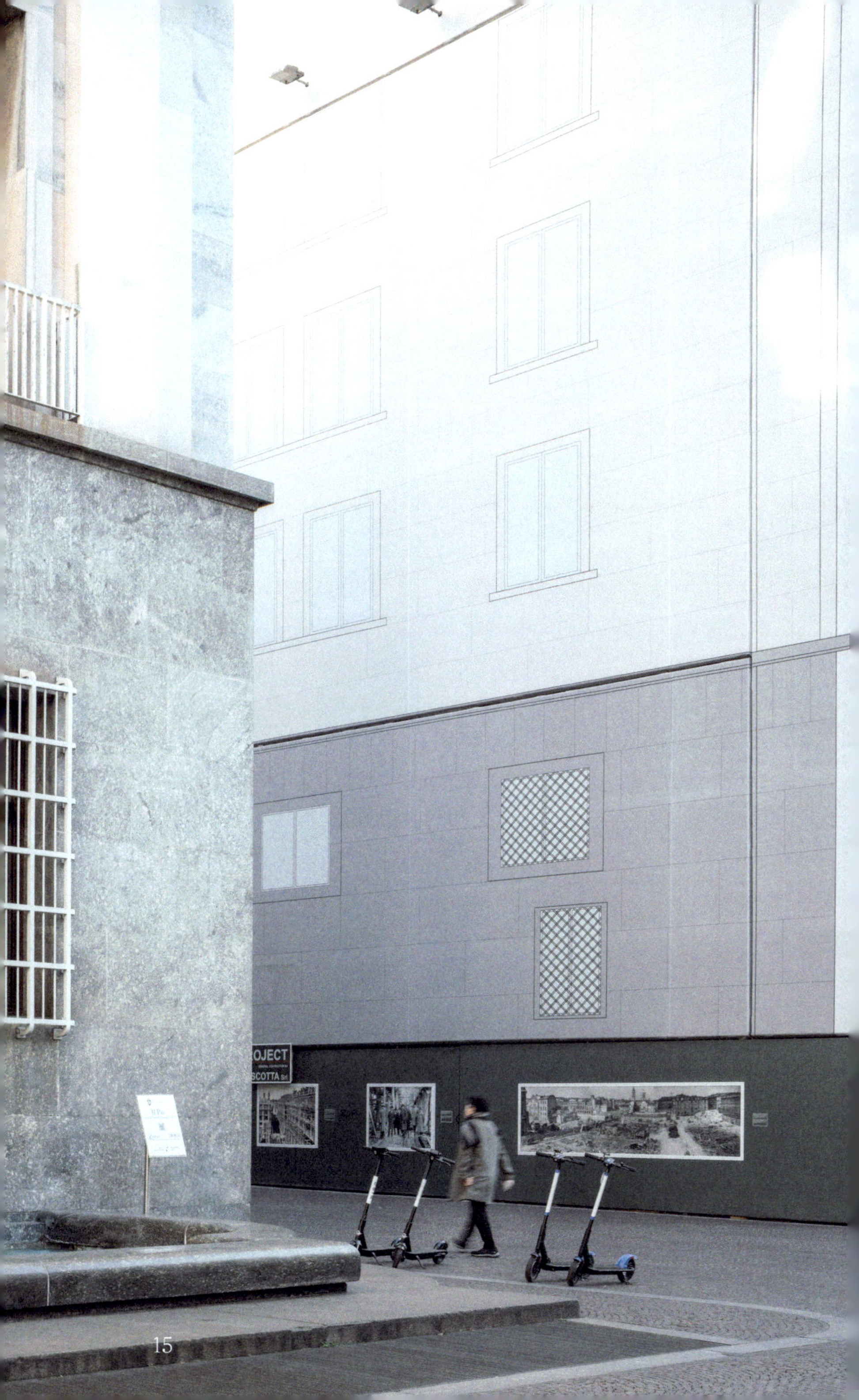
OJECT
SCOTTA

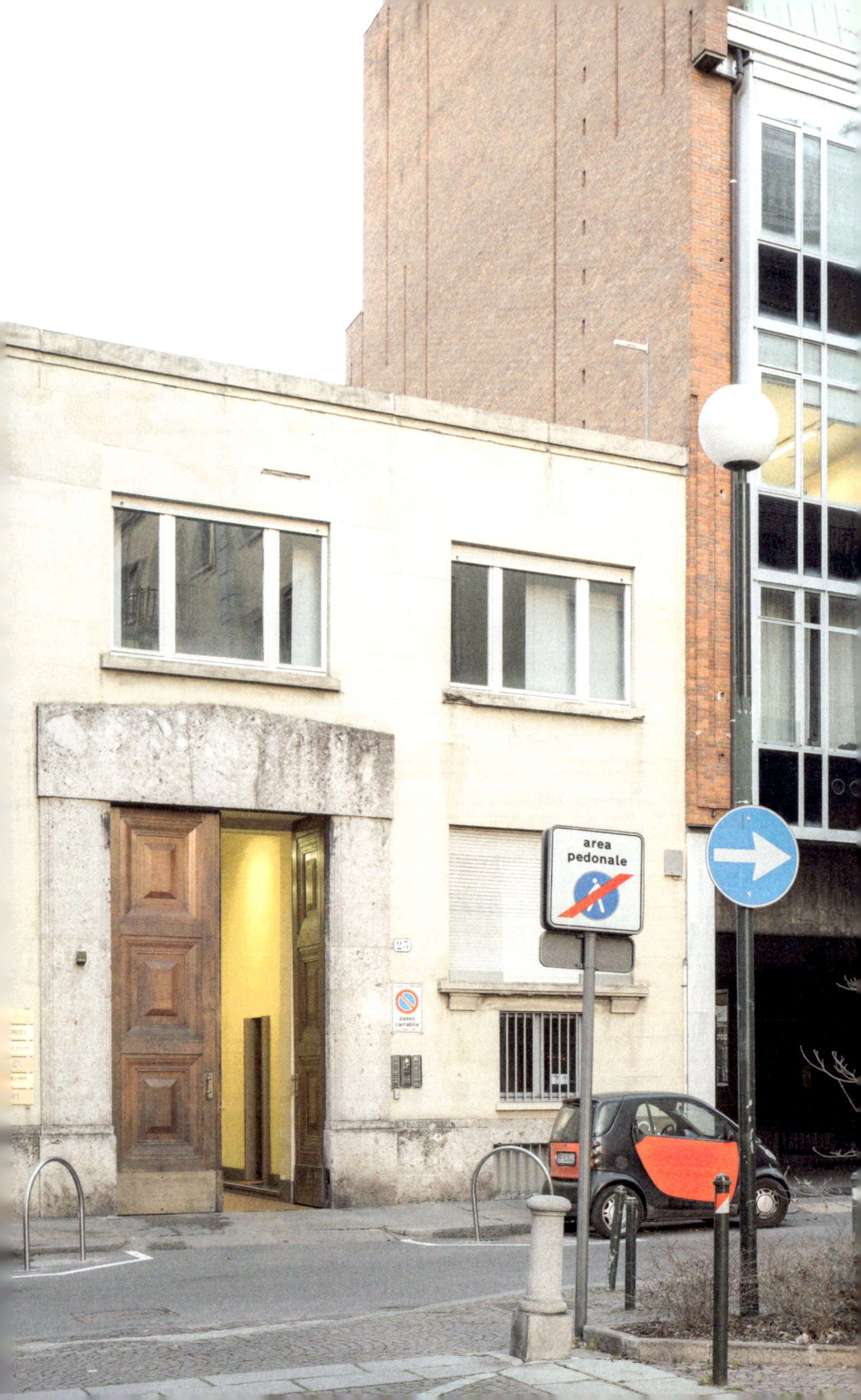
area
pedonale
passo
carrabile

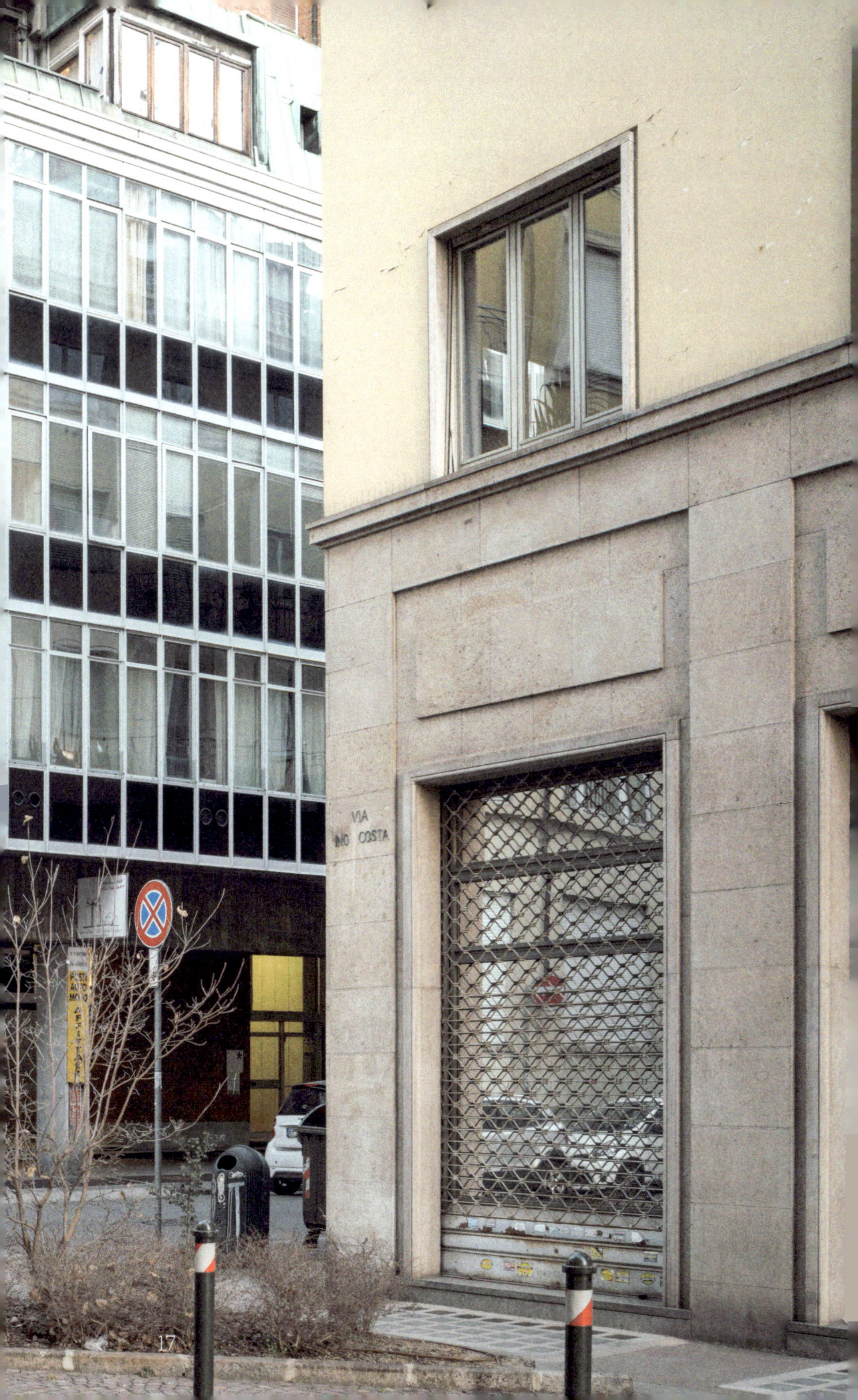
VIA
INO COSTA

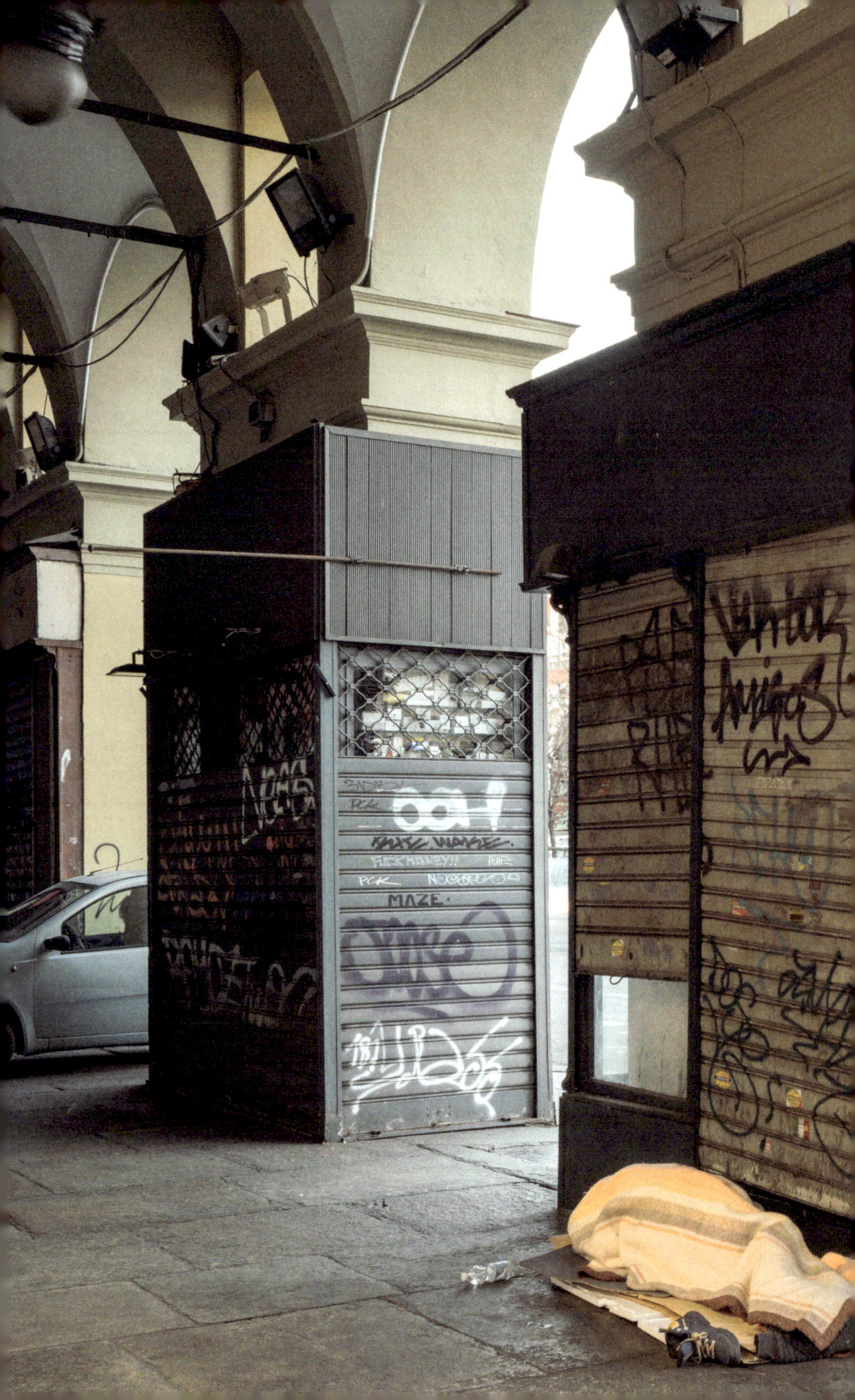
PCK
FUCK MONEY!!
PCK
MAZE.

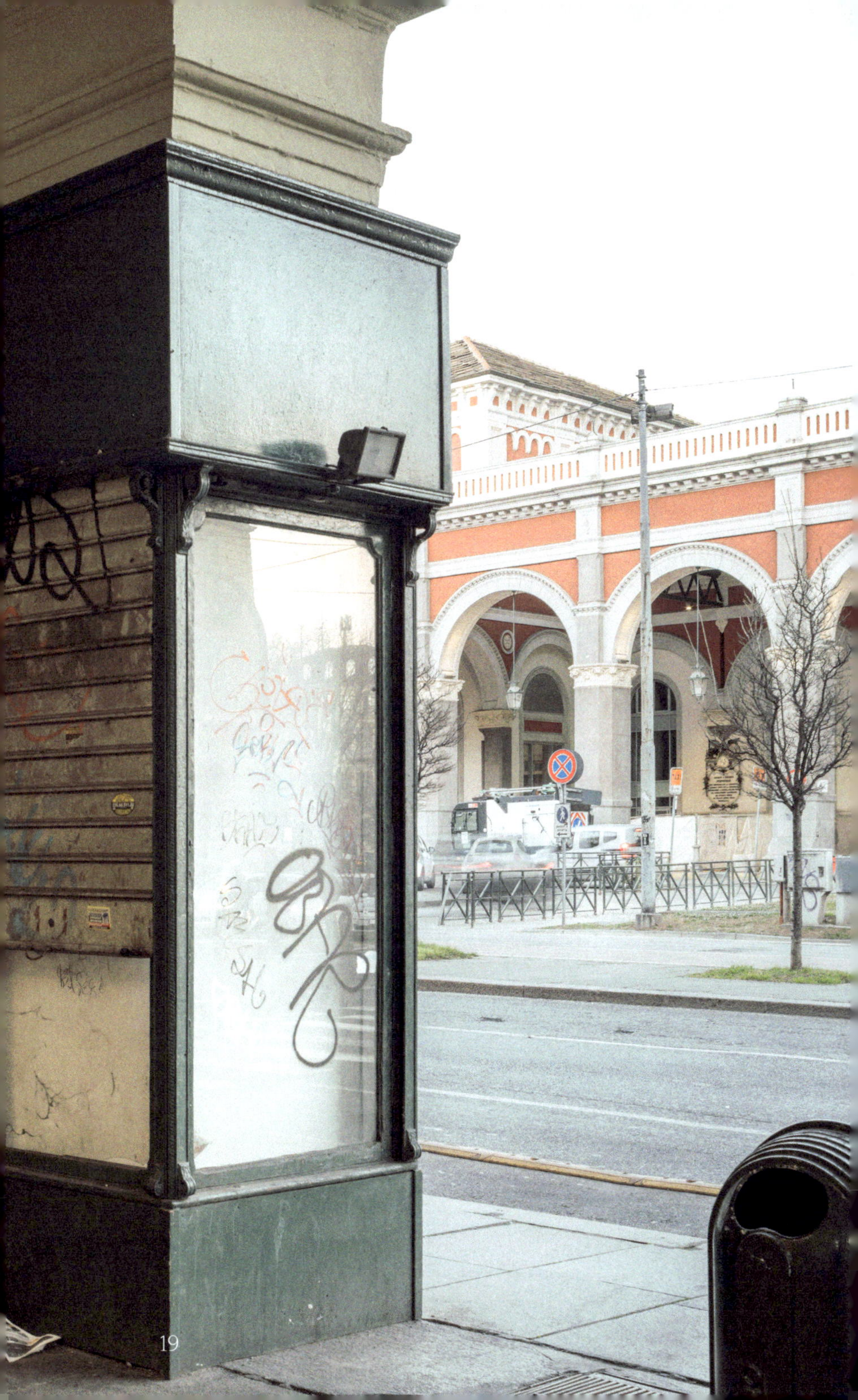

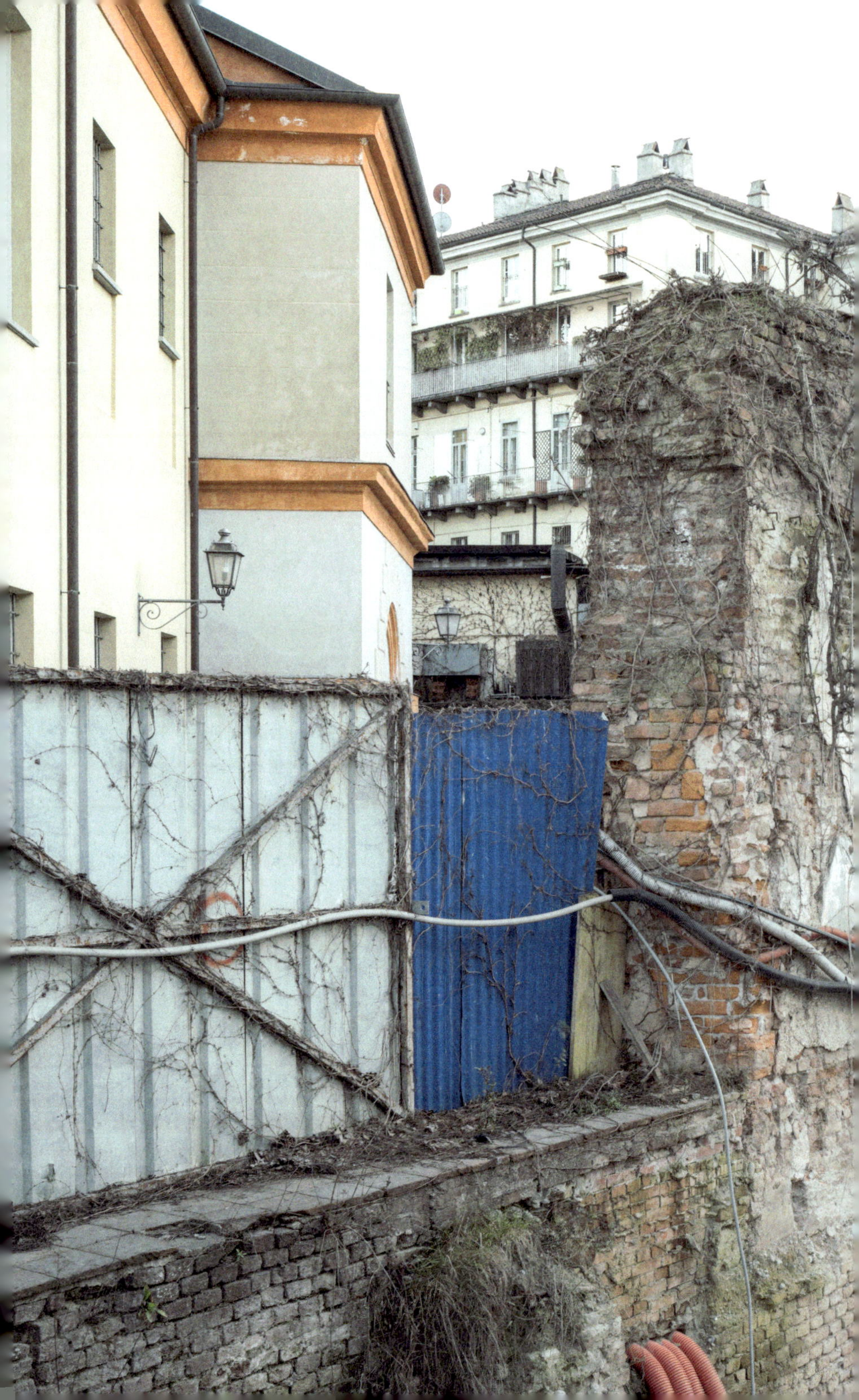

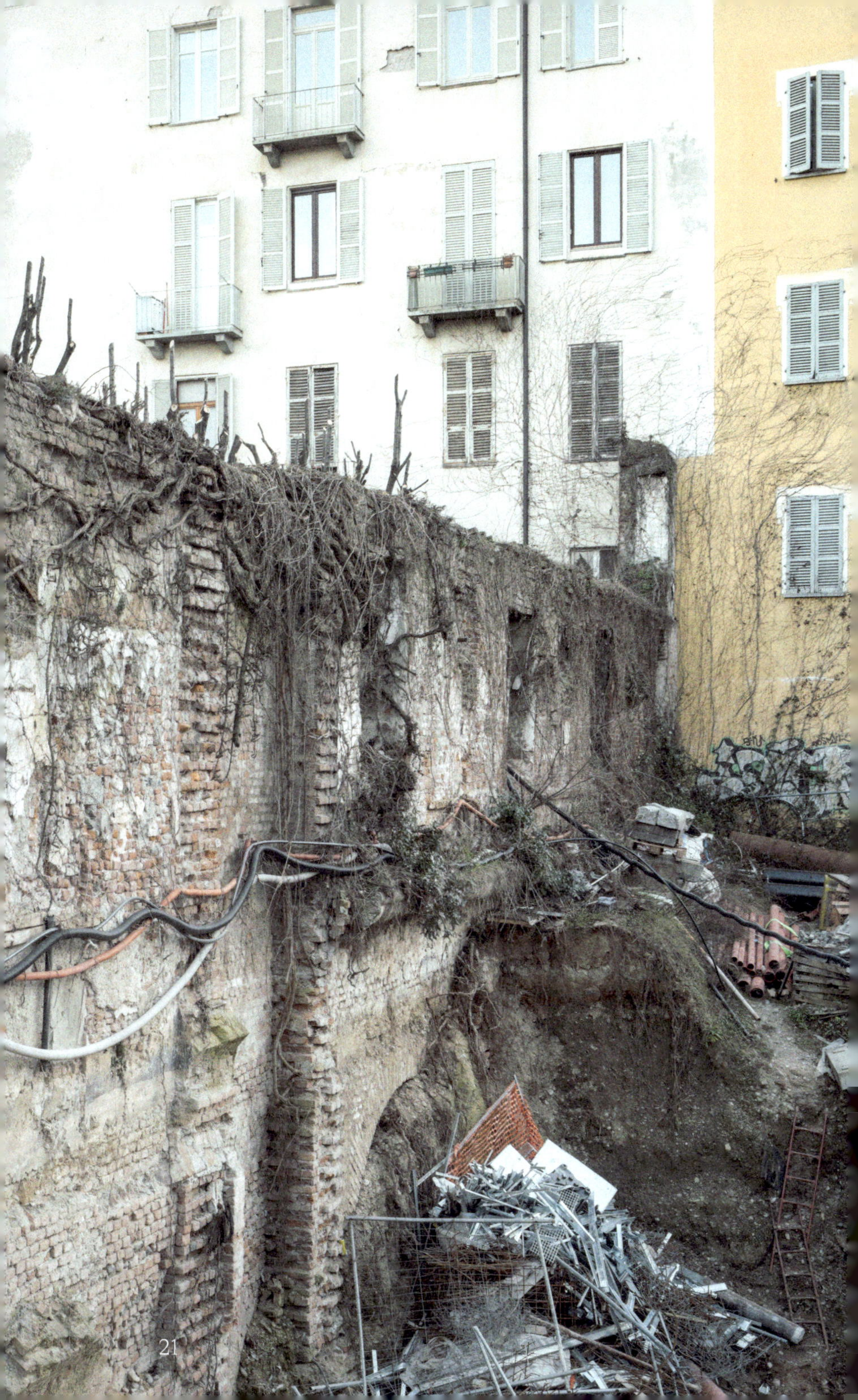

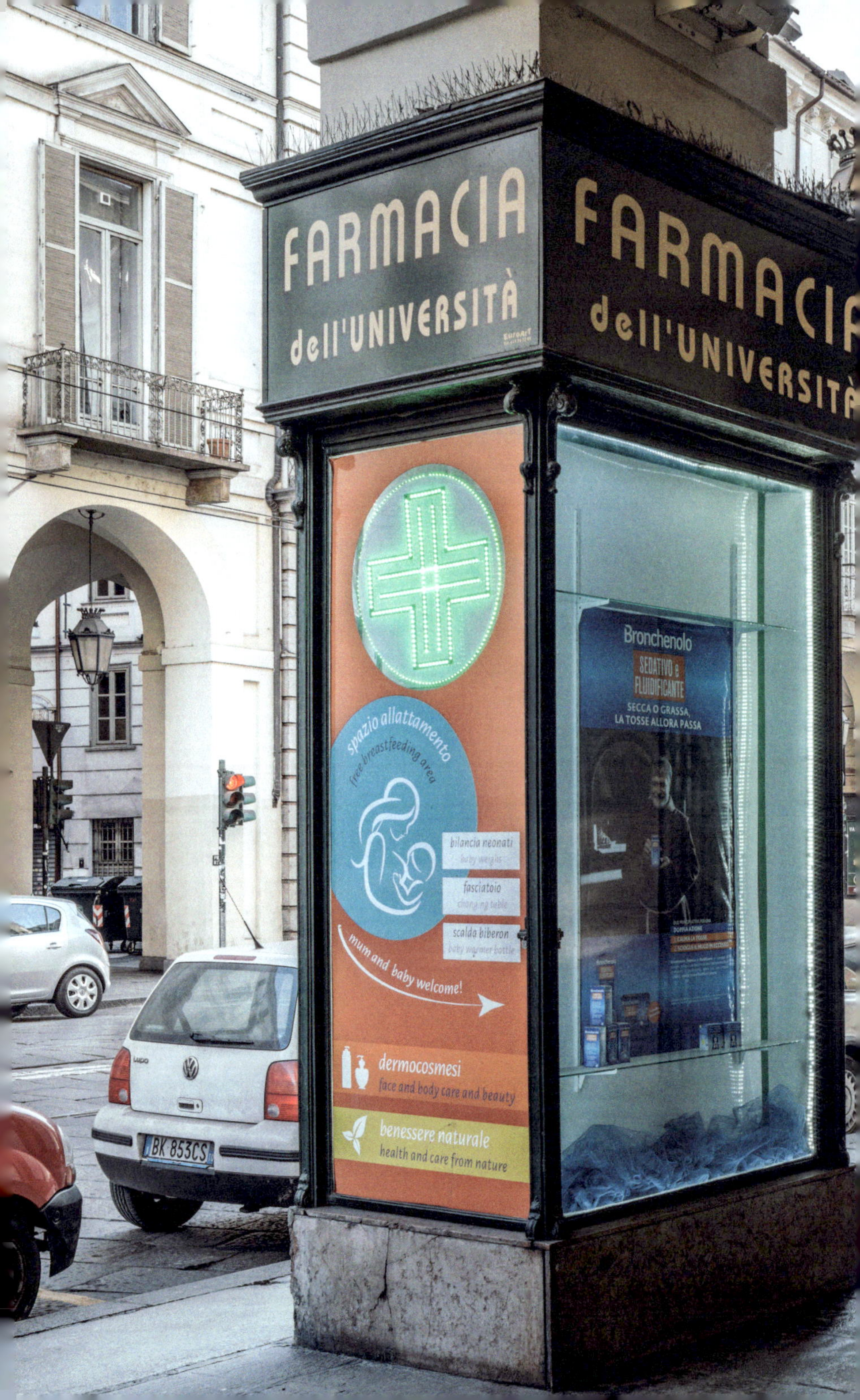
FARMACIA
dell'UNIVERSITÀ
FARMACIA
dell'UNIVERSITÀ
spazio allattamento
free breastfeeding area
bilancia neonati
fasciatoio
changing table
scalda biberon
baby warmer bottle
mum and baby welcome!
dermocosmesi
face and body care and beauty
benessere naturale
health and care from nature
Bronchenolo
SEDATIVO e FLUIDIFICANTE
SECCA O GRASSA,
LA TOSSE ALLORA PASSA
BK 853CS

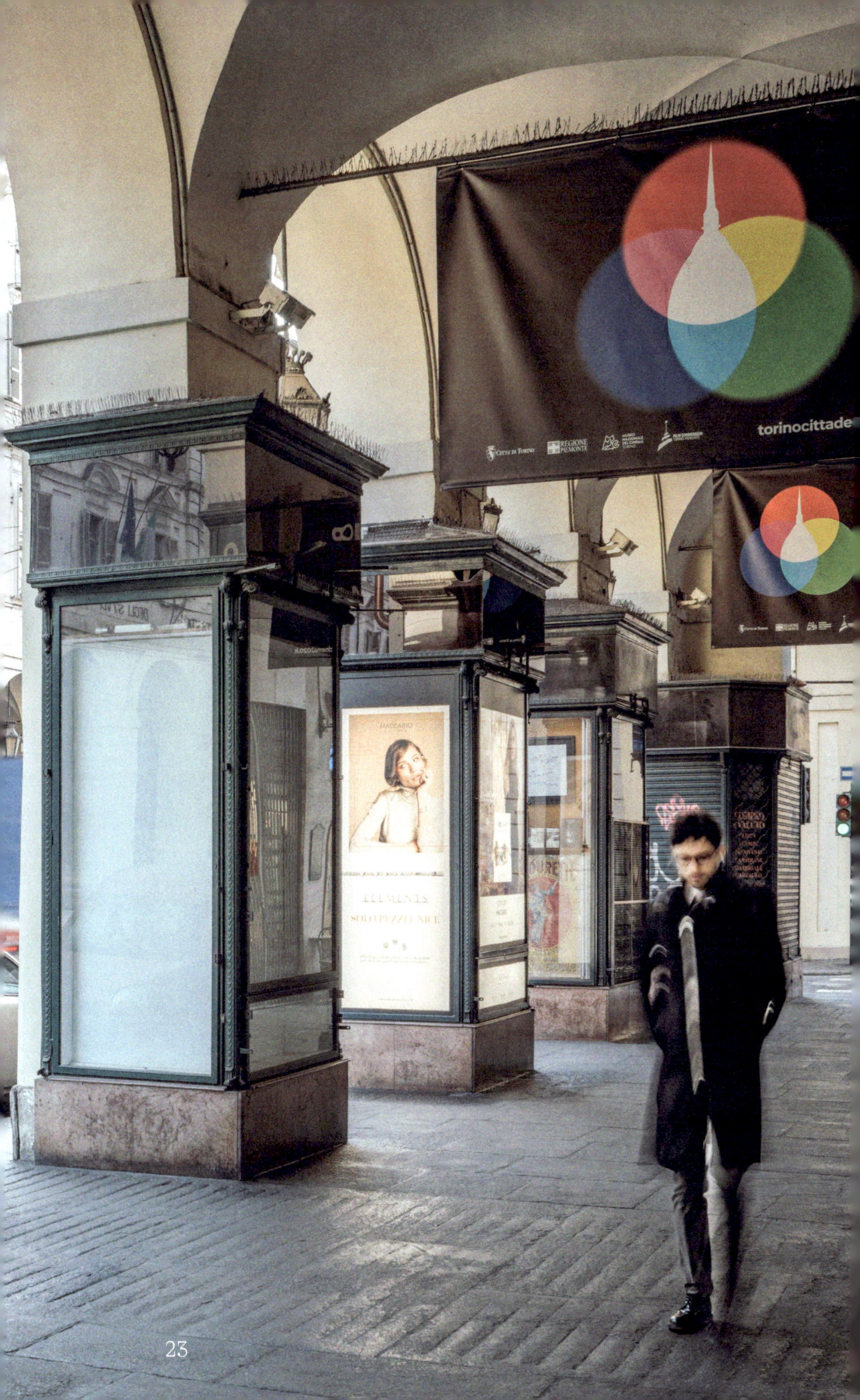
torinocittade
REGIONE
PIEMONTE

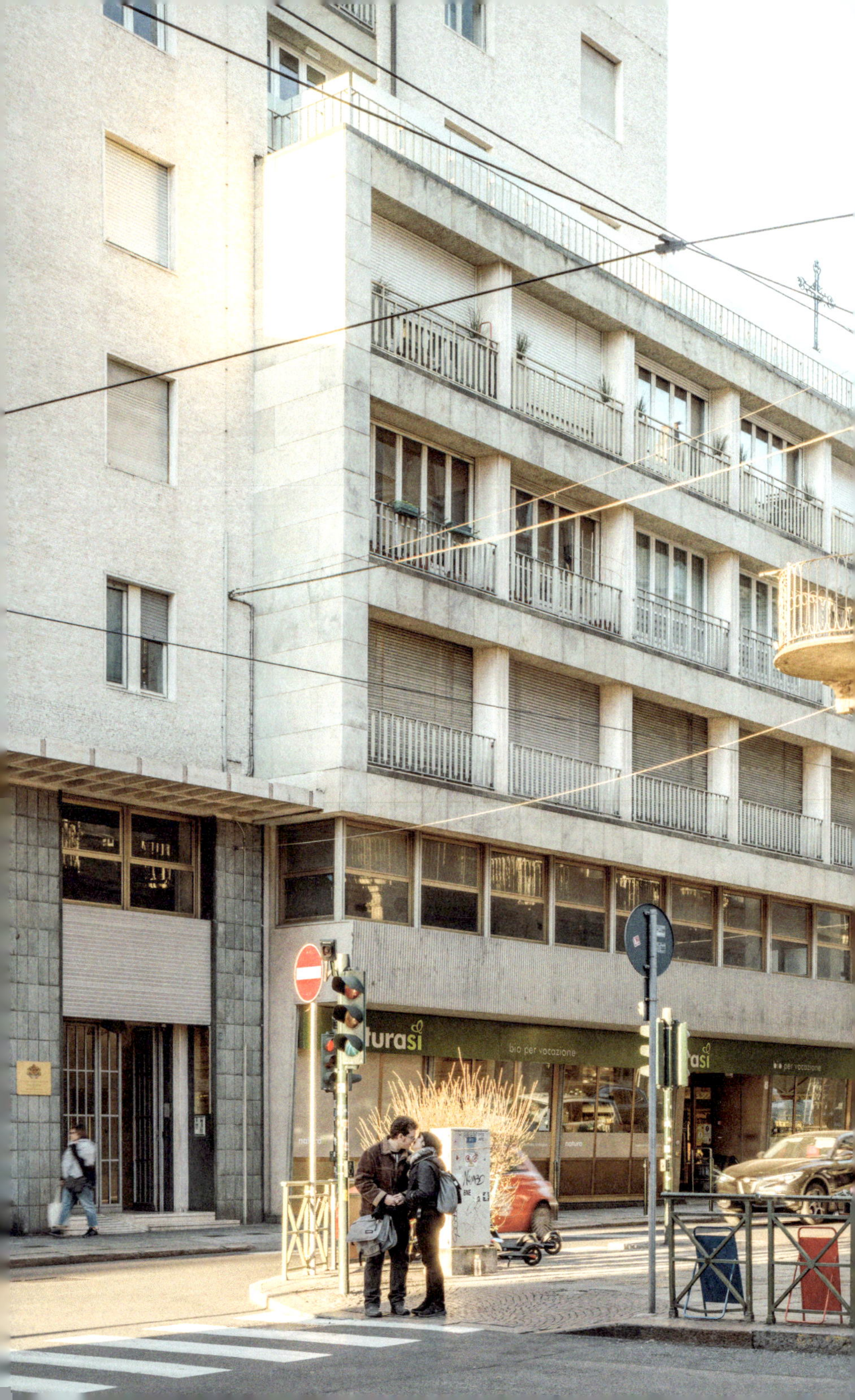
bio per vocazione

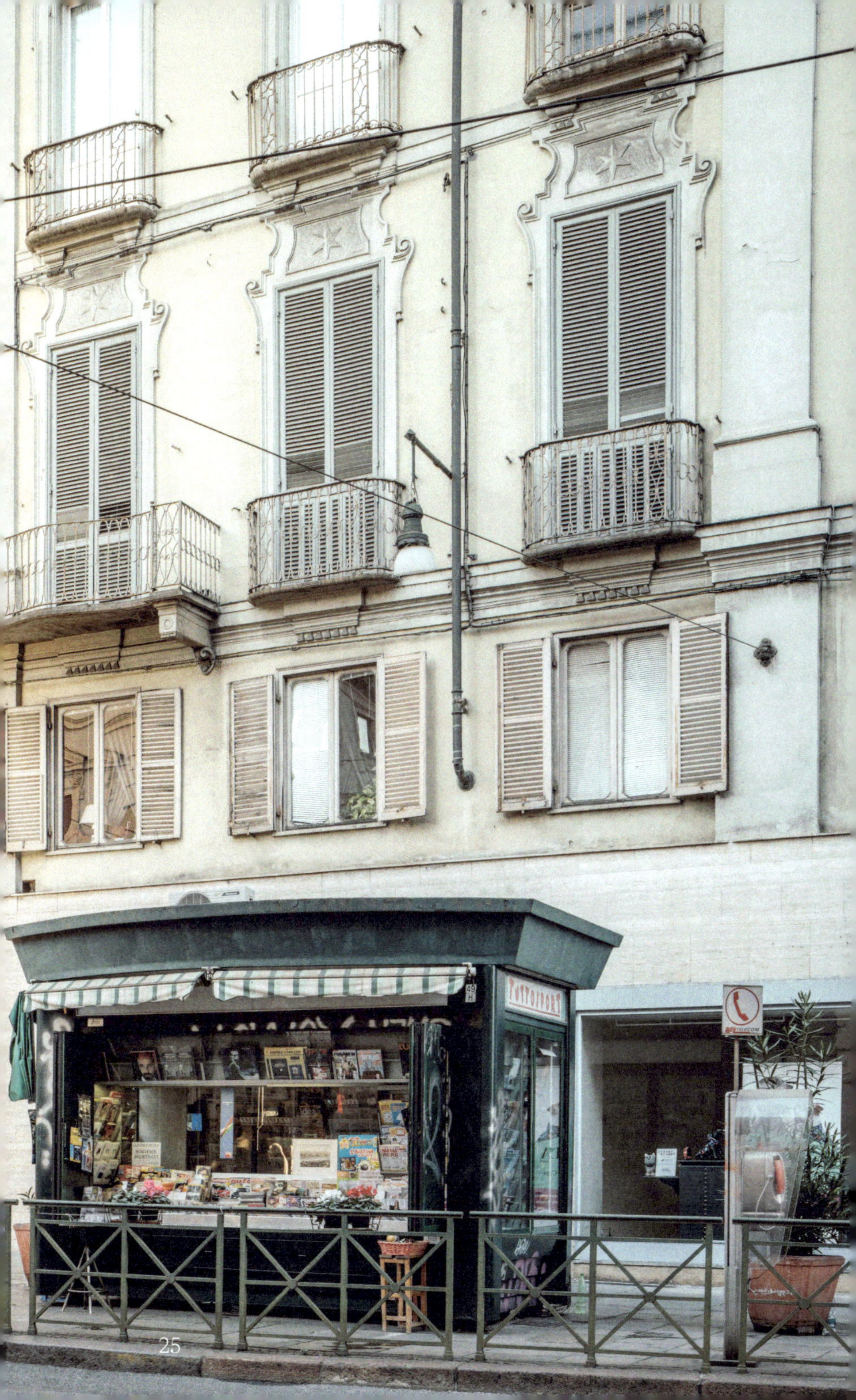

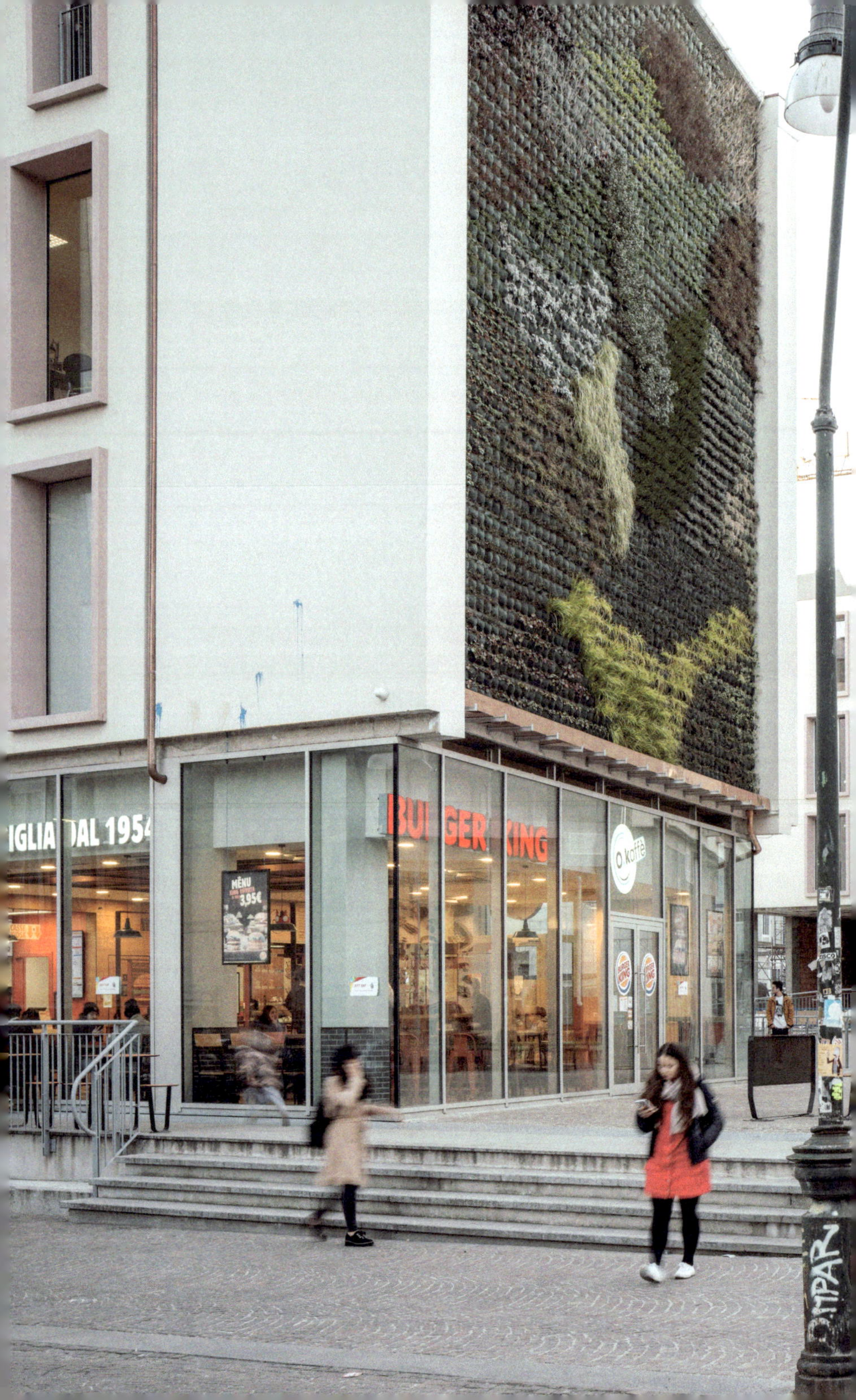

DAL 1954
BURGER KING
MENU
3,95€

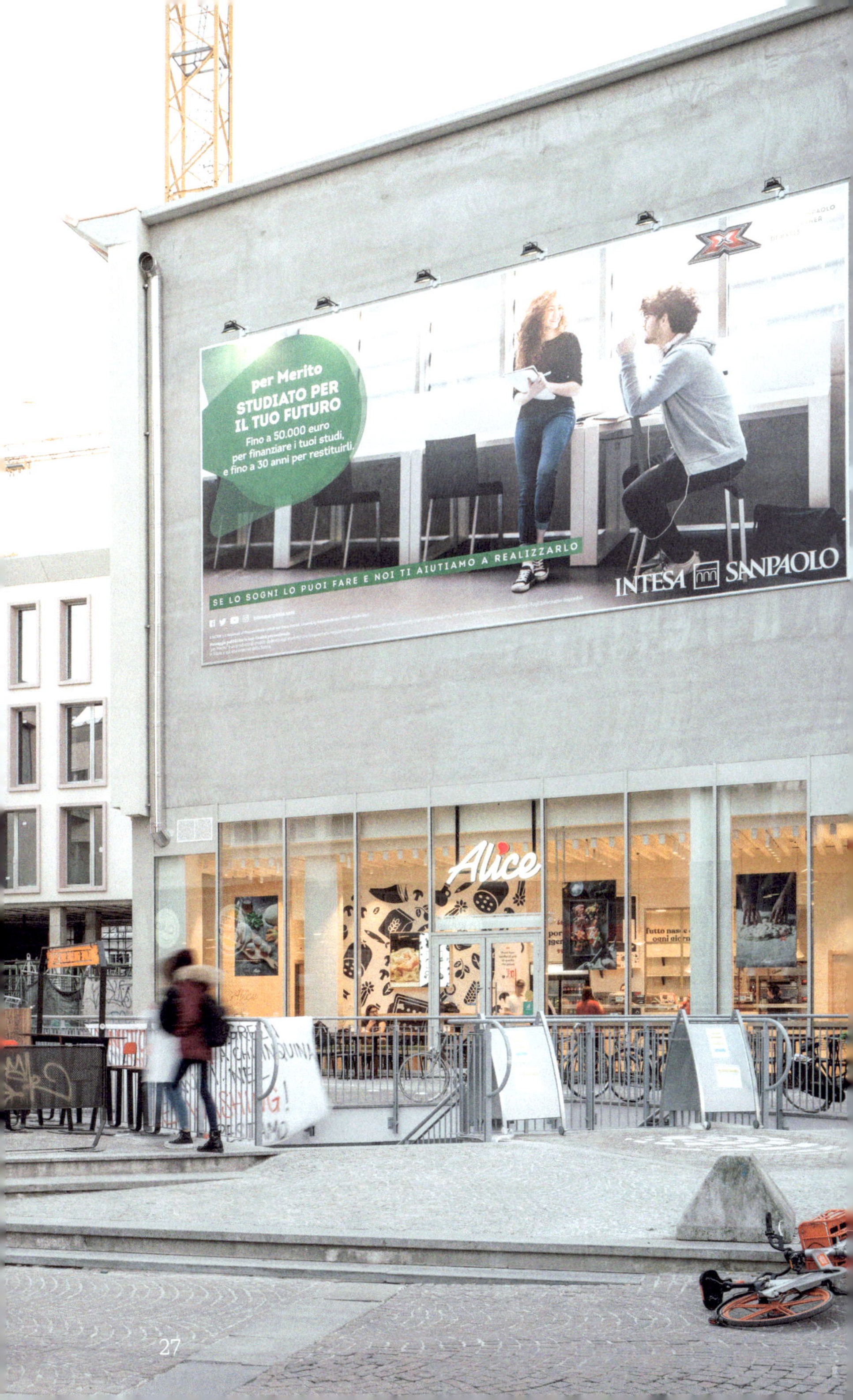
per Merito
STUDIATO PER
IL TUO FUTURO
Fino a 50.000 euro
per finanziare i tuoi studi,
e fino a 30 anni per restituirli.
SE LO SOGNI LO PUOI FARE E NOI TI AIUTIAMO A REALIZZARLO
INTESA SANPAOLO
Alice

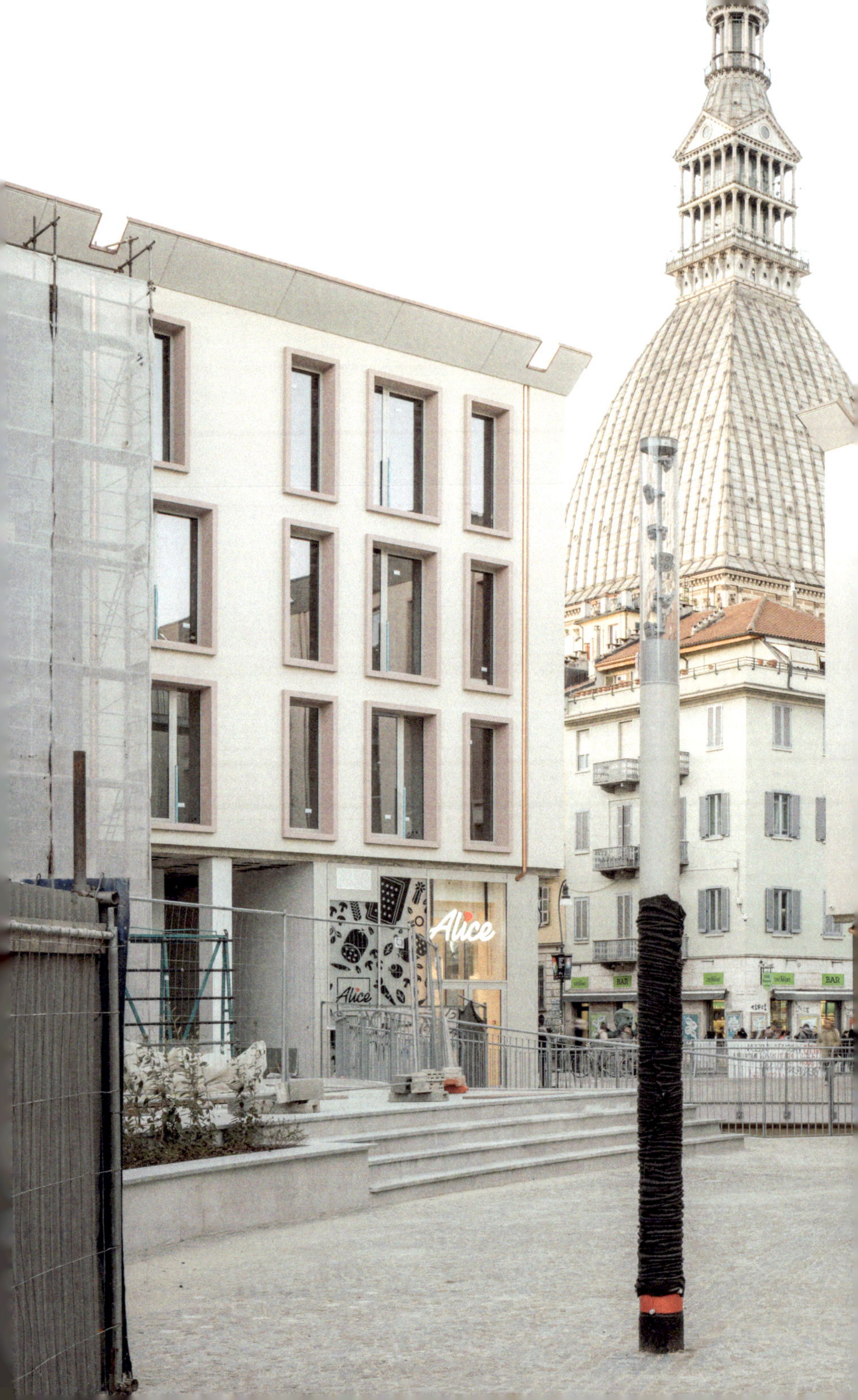
Alice
Alice
BAR
BAR

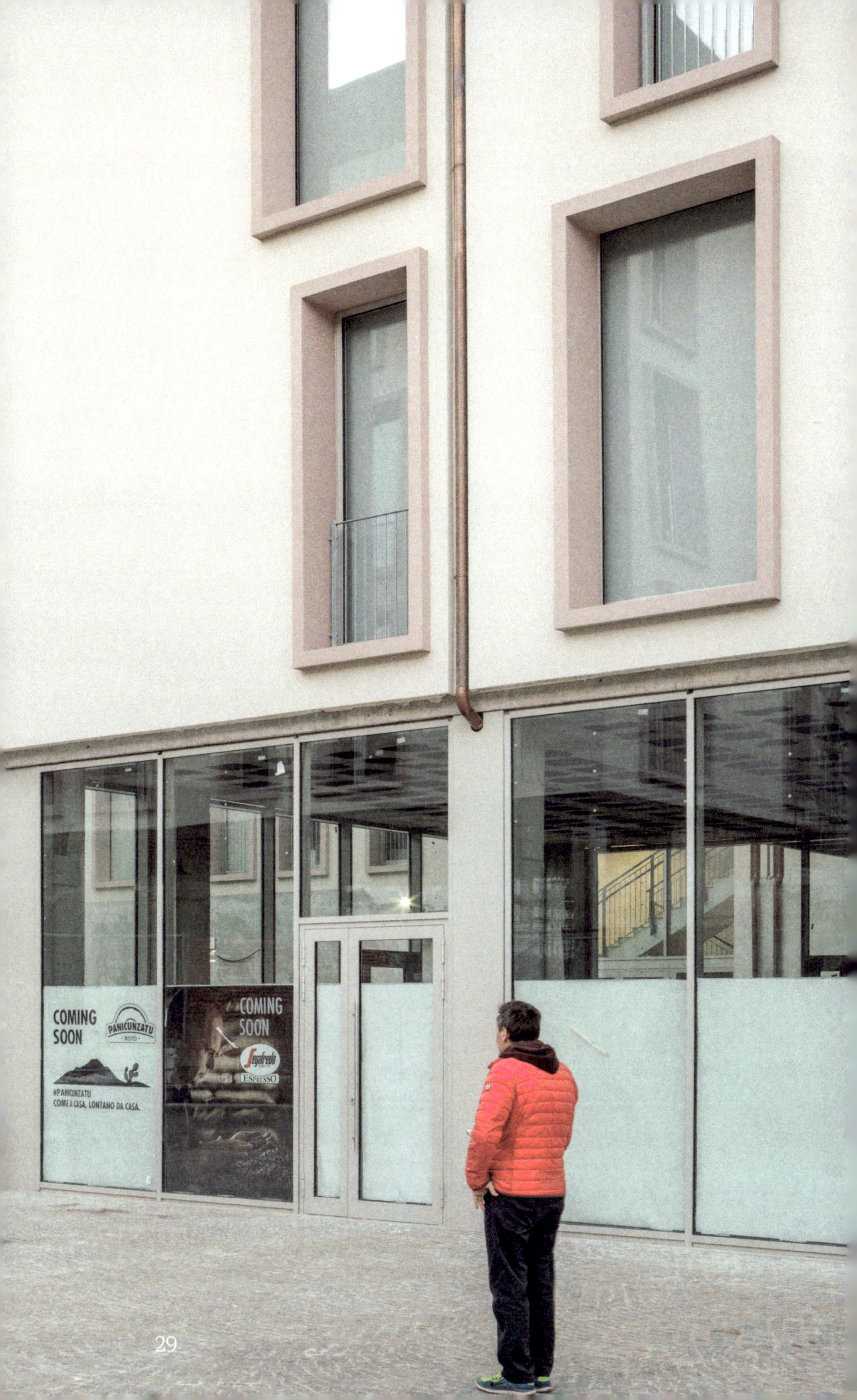
COMING SOON
PANICUNZATU
RISTO
#PANICUNZATU
COME A CASA, LONTANO DA CASA.
COMING SOON
Segafredo
ESPRESSO

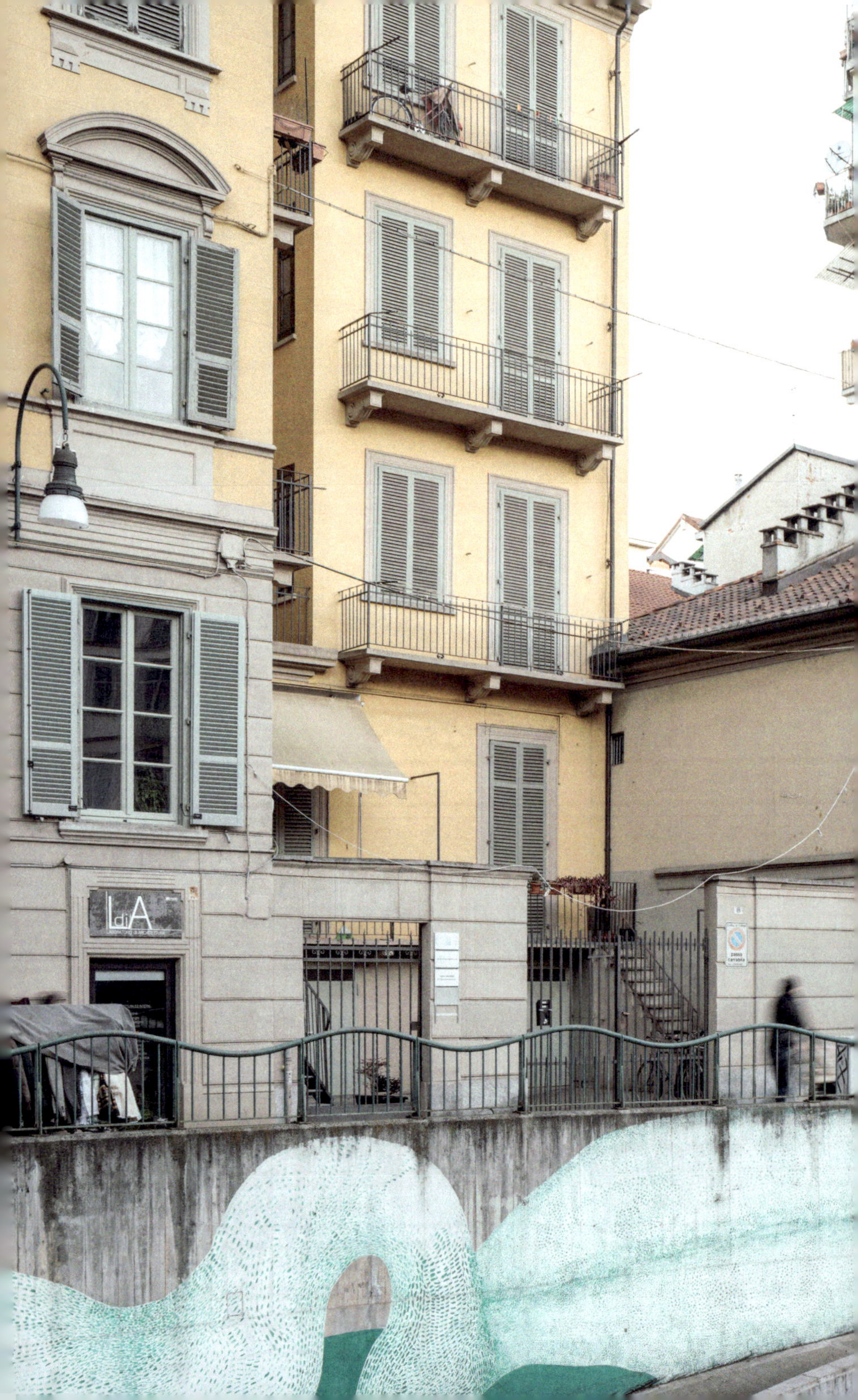
LdiA

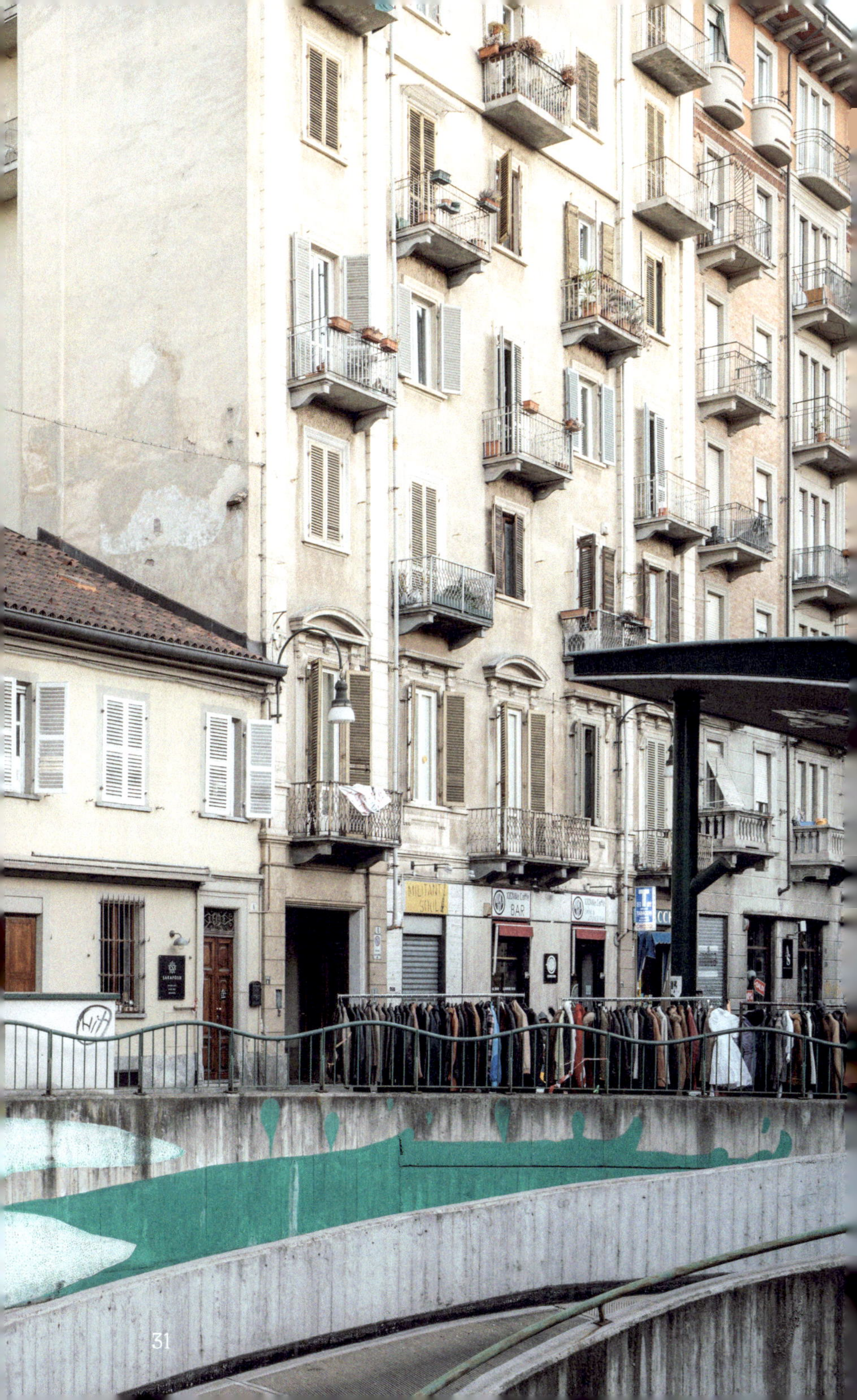
MILITANT SOIL
BAR

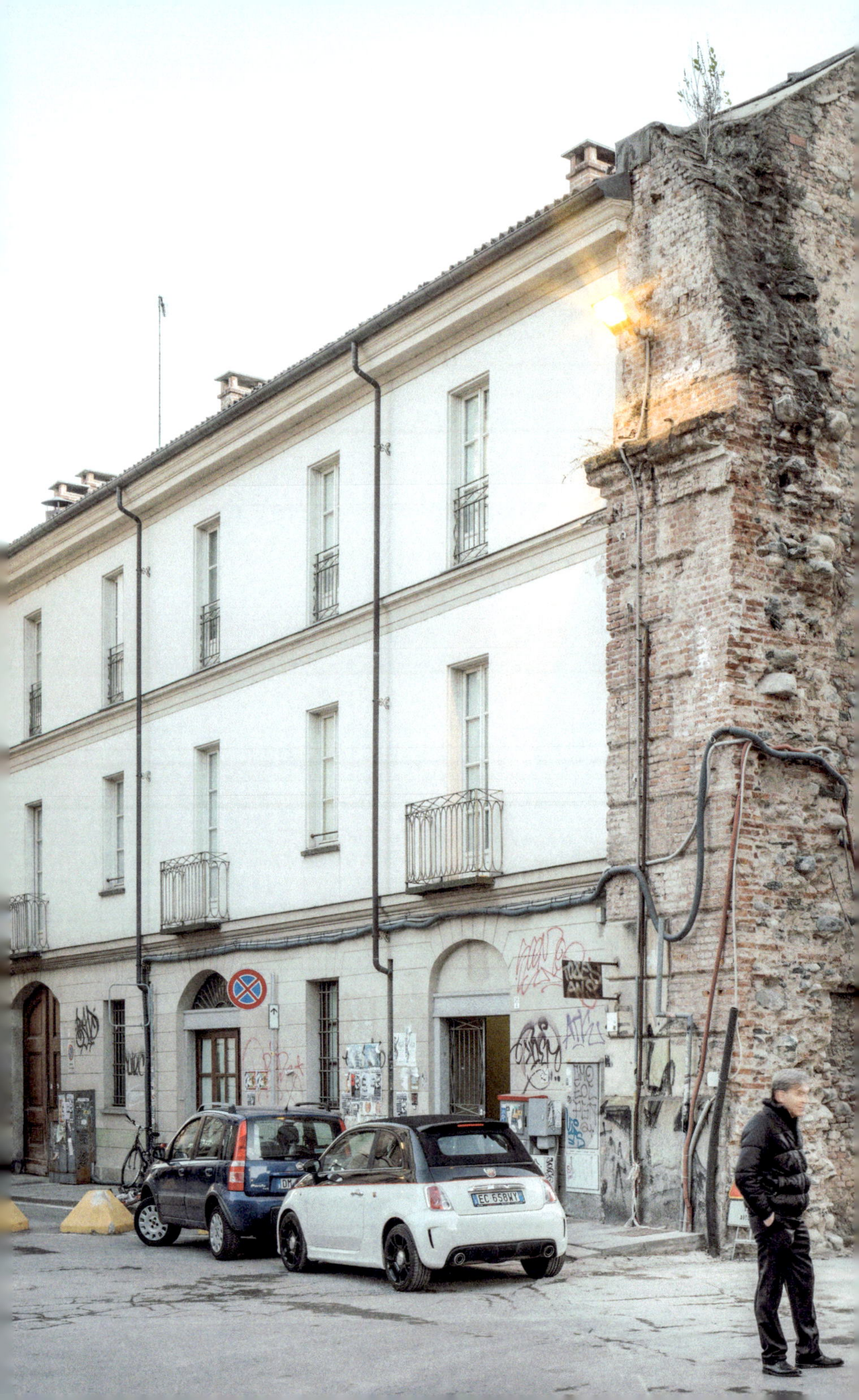
EC 658WY

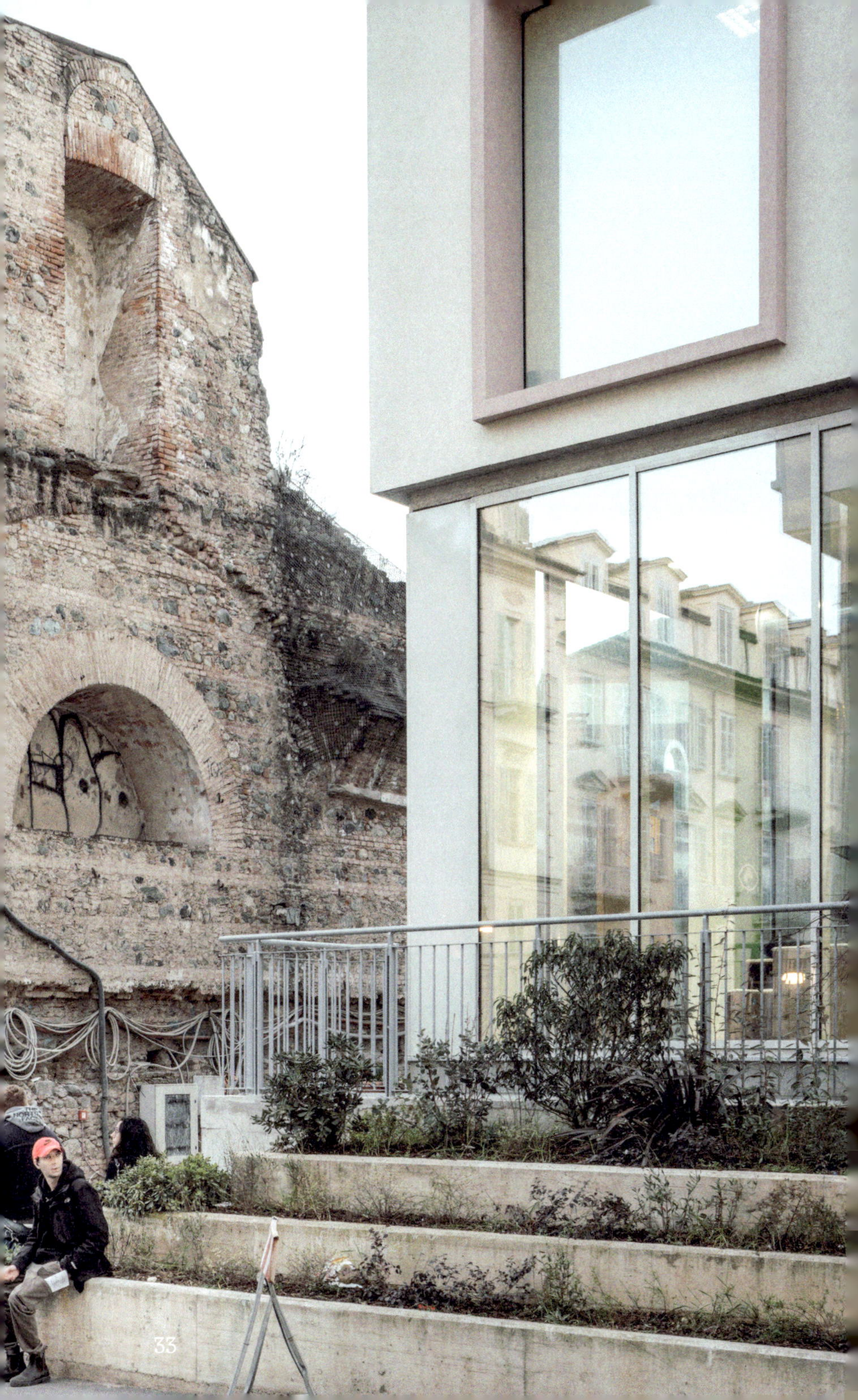

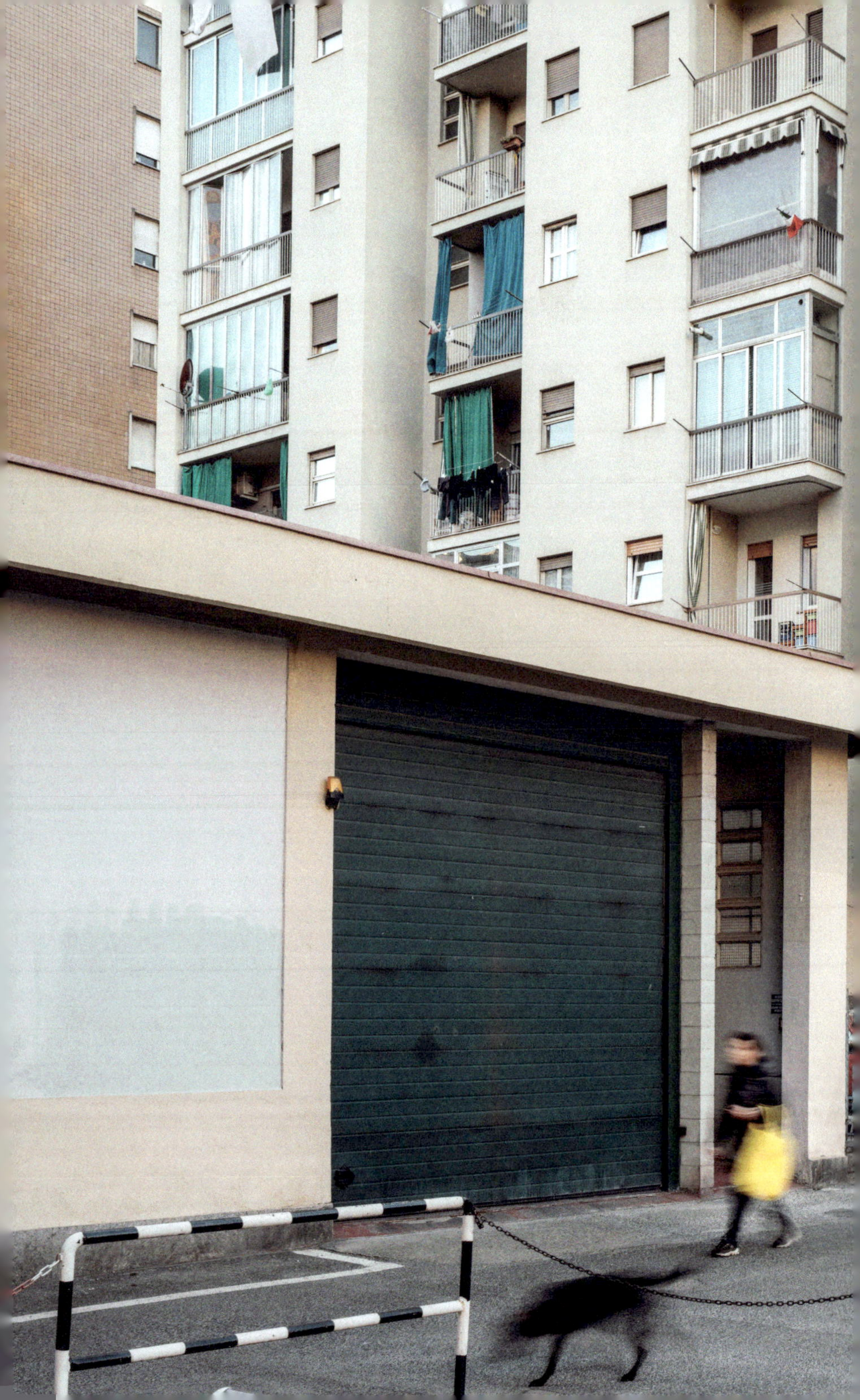

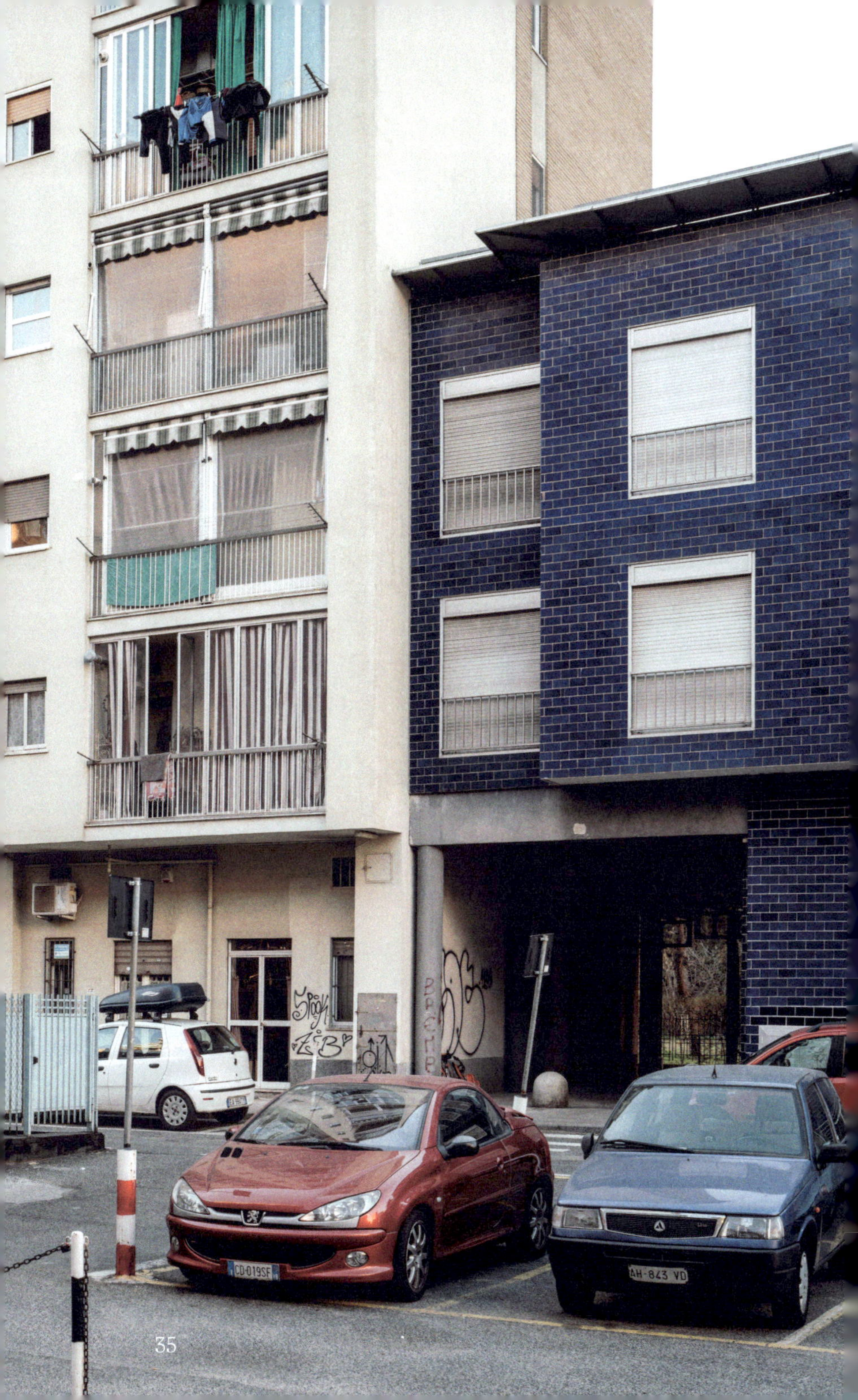
CD·019SF
AH·843 VD

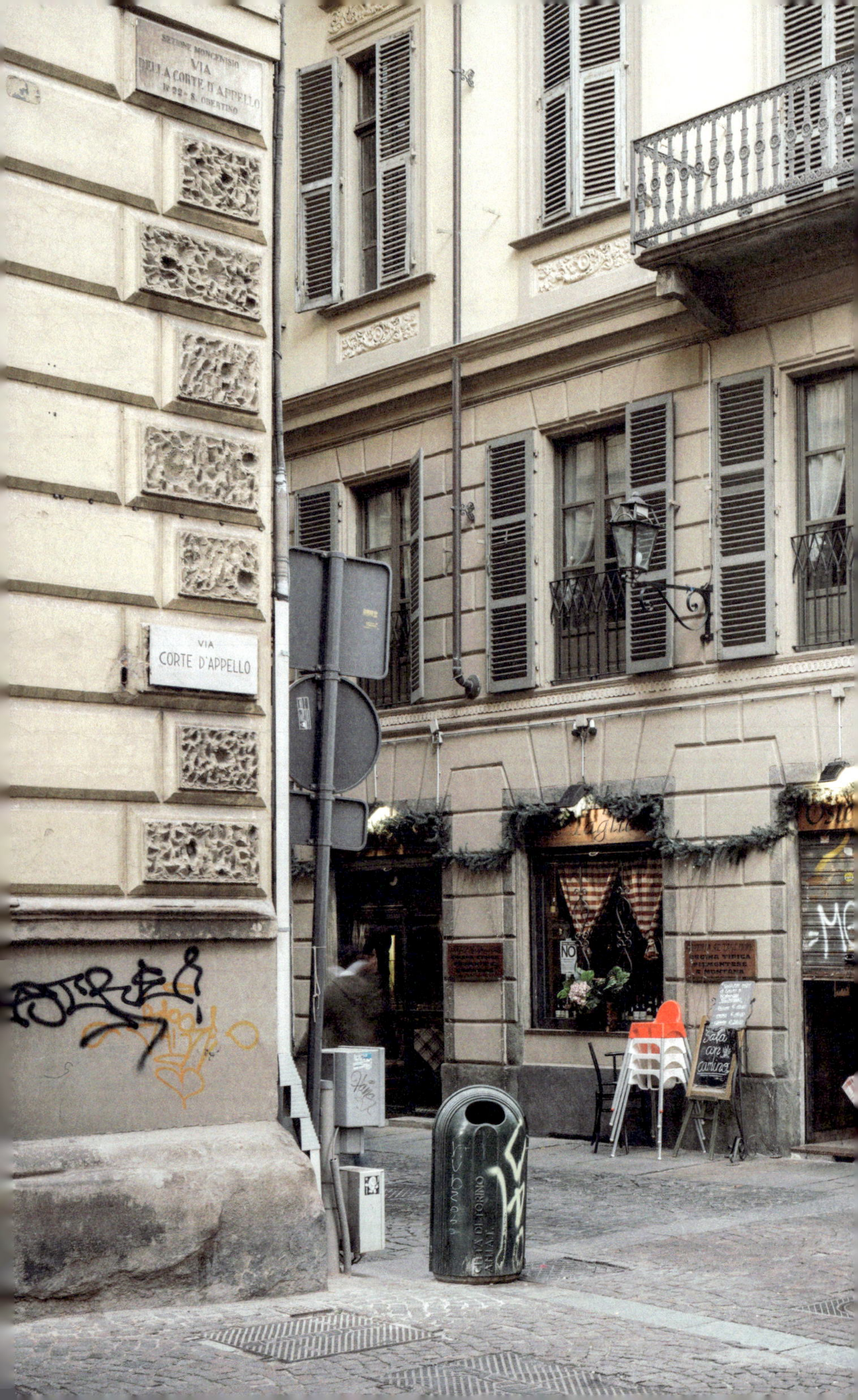
MONCENISIO
VIA
DELLA CORTE D'APPELLO
S. OBERTINO
VIA
CORTE D'APPELLO

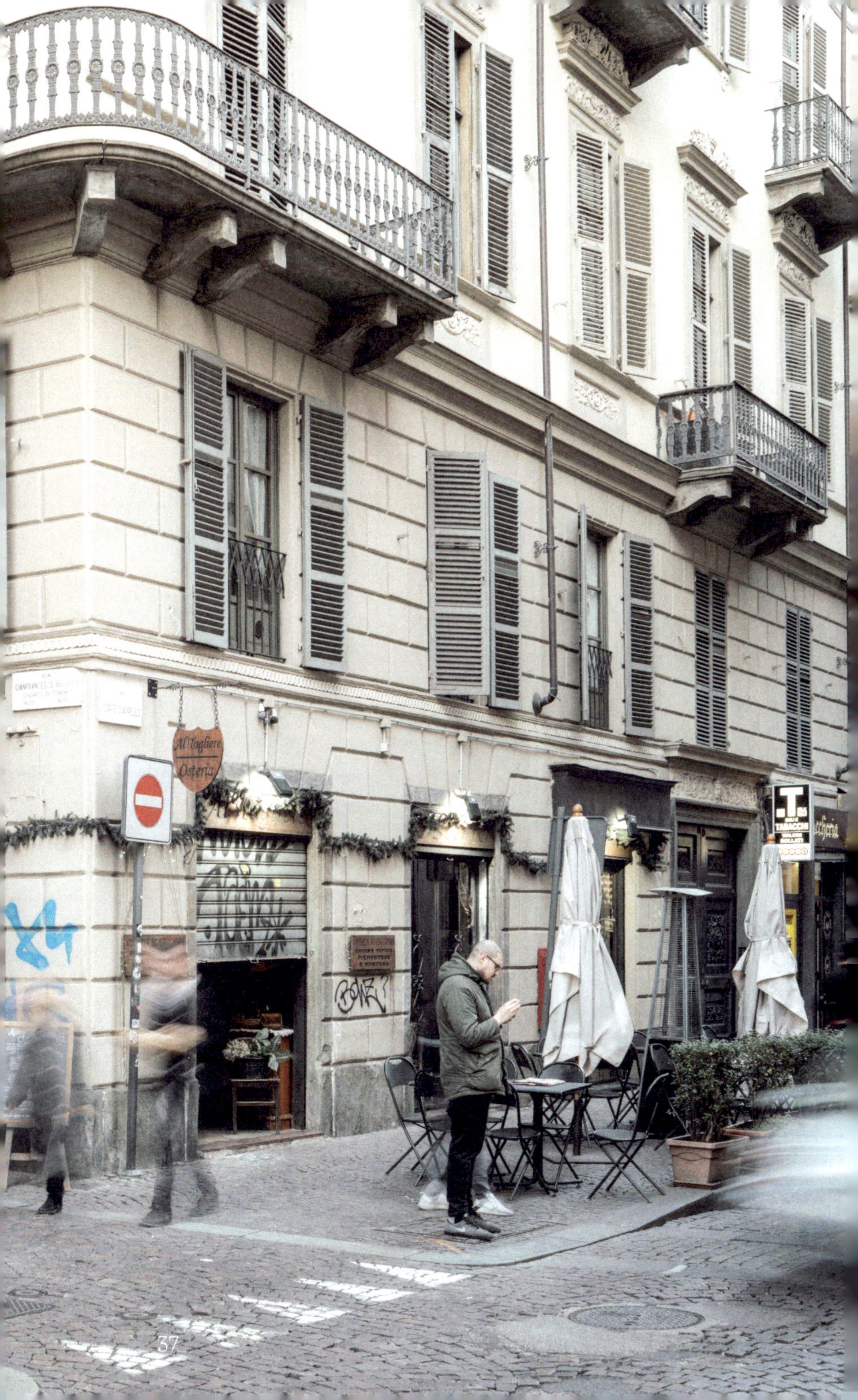
VIA
CORTE D'APPELLO
Al Tagliere
Osteria
TABACCHI

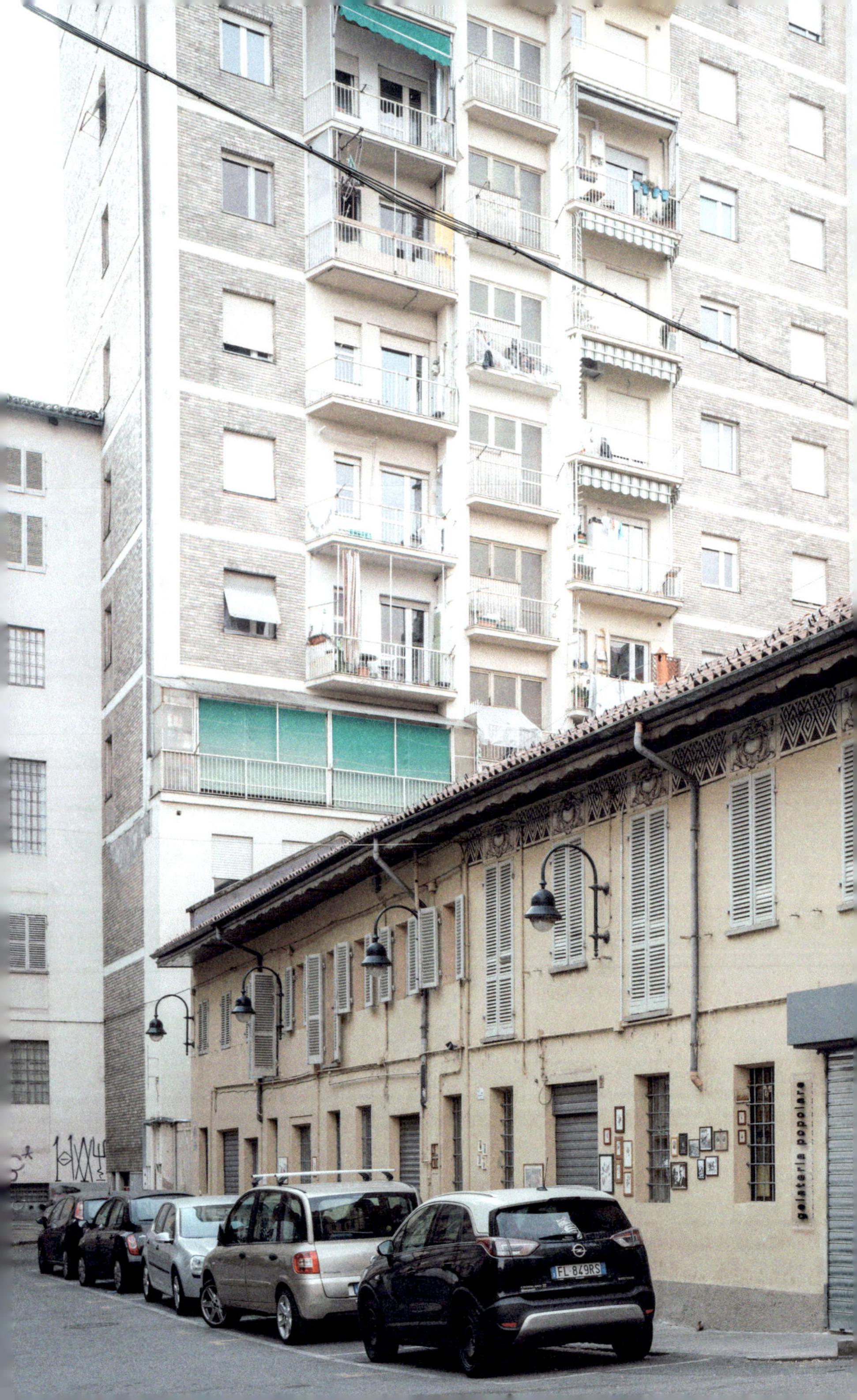
gelateria popolare
FL 849RS

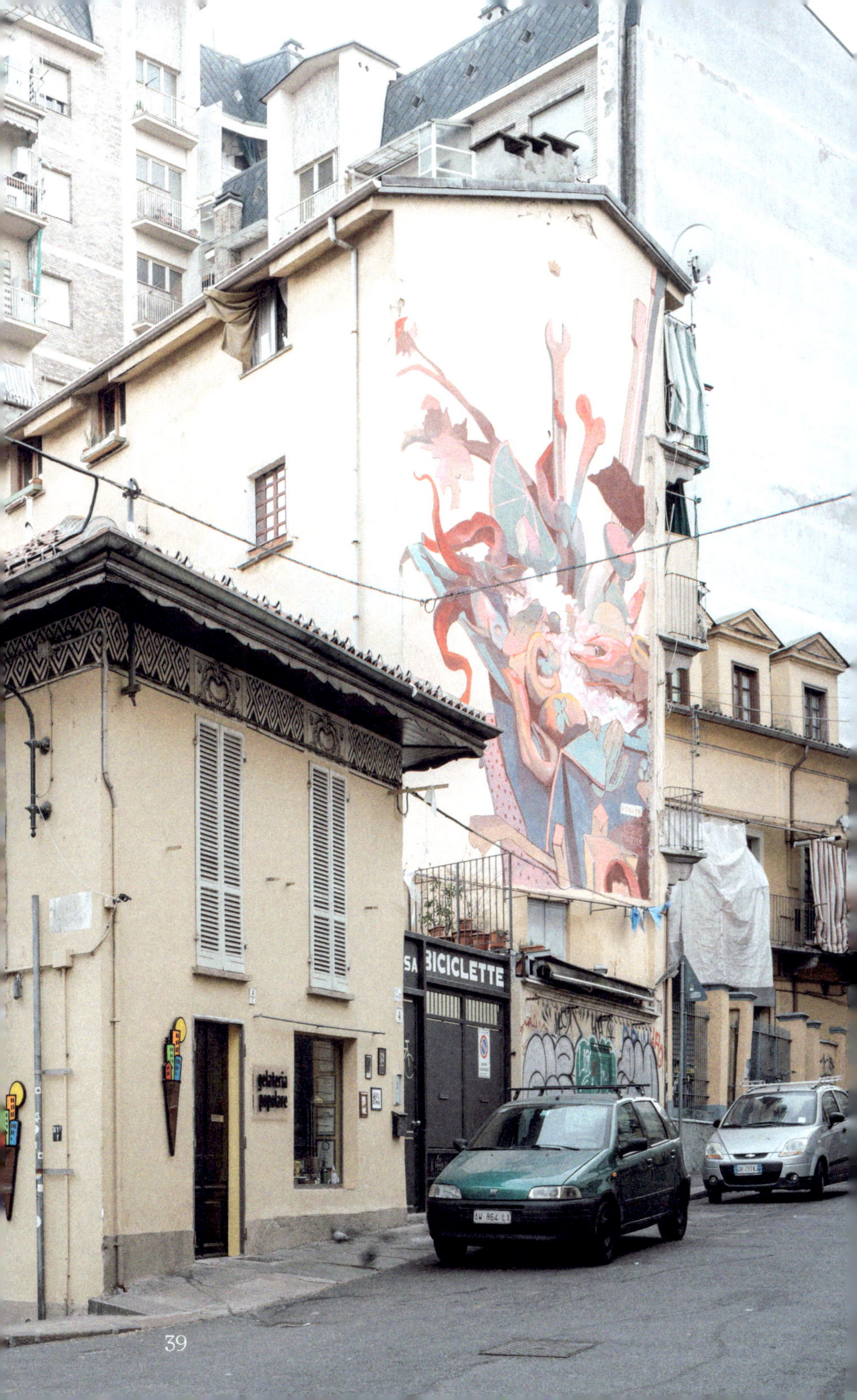
BICICLETTE
gelateria
popolare

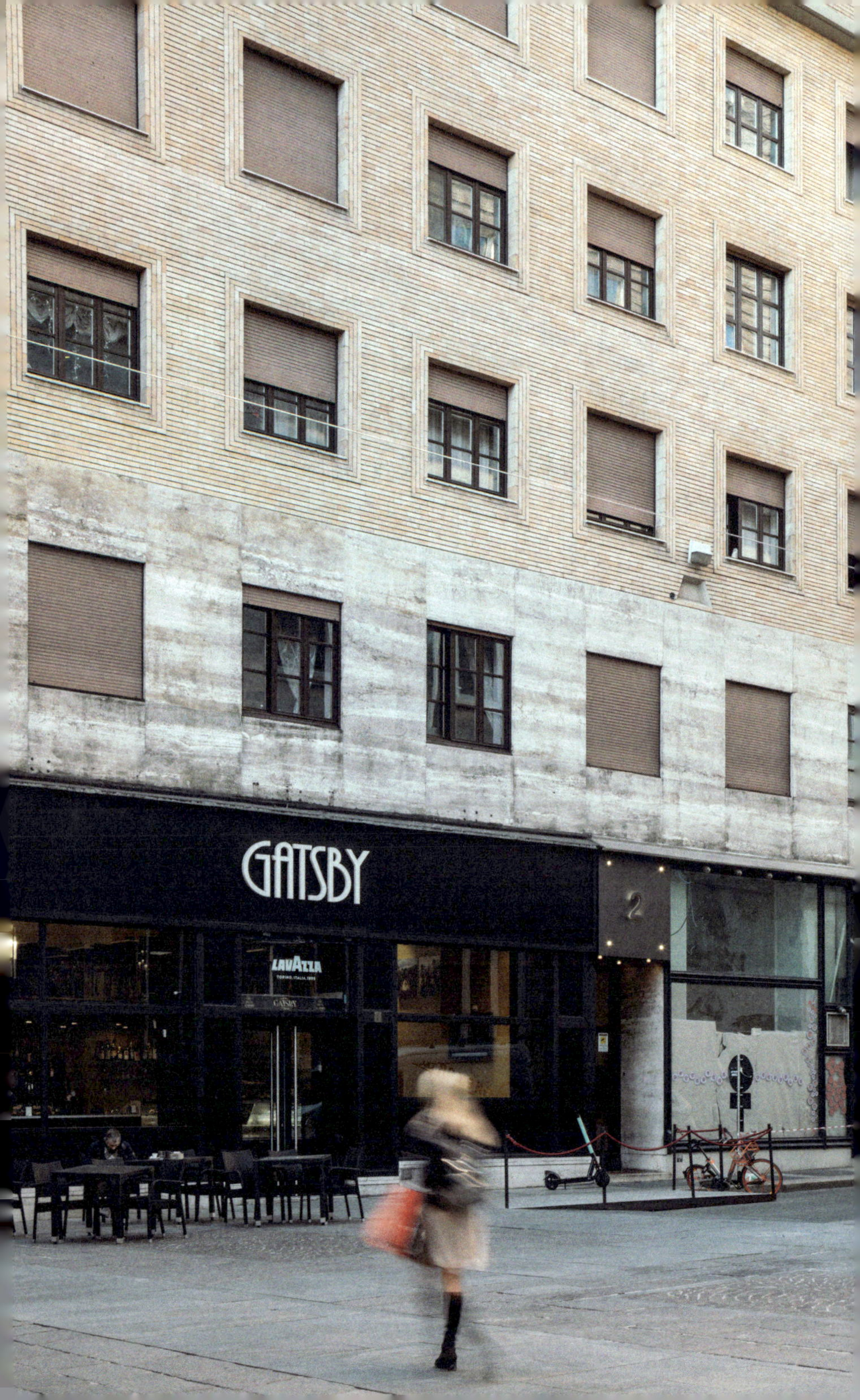
GATSBY
LAVAZZA

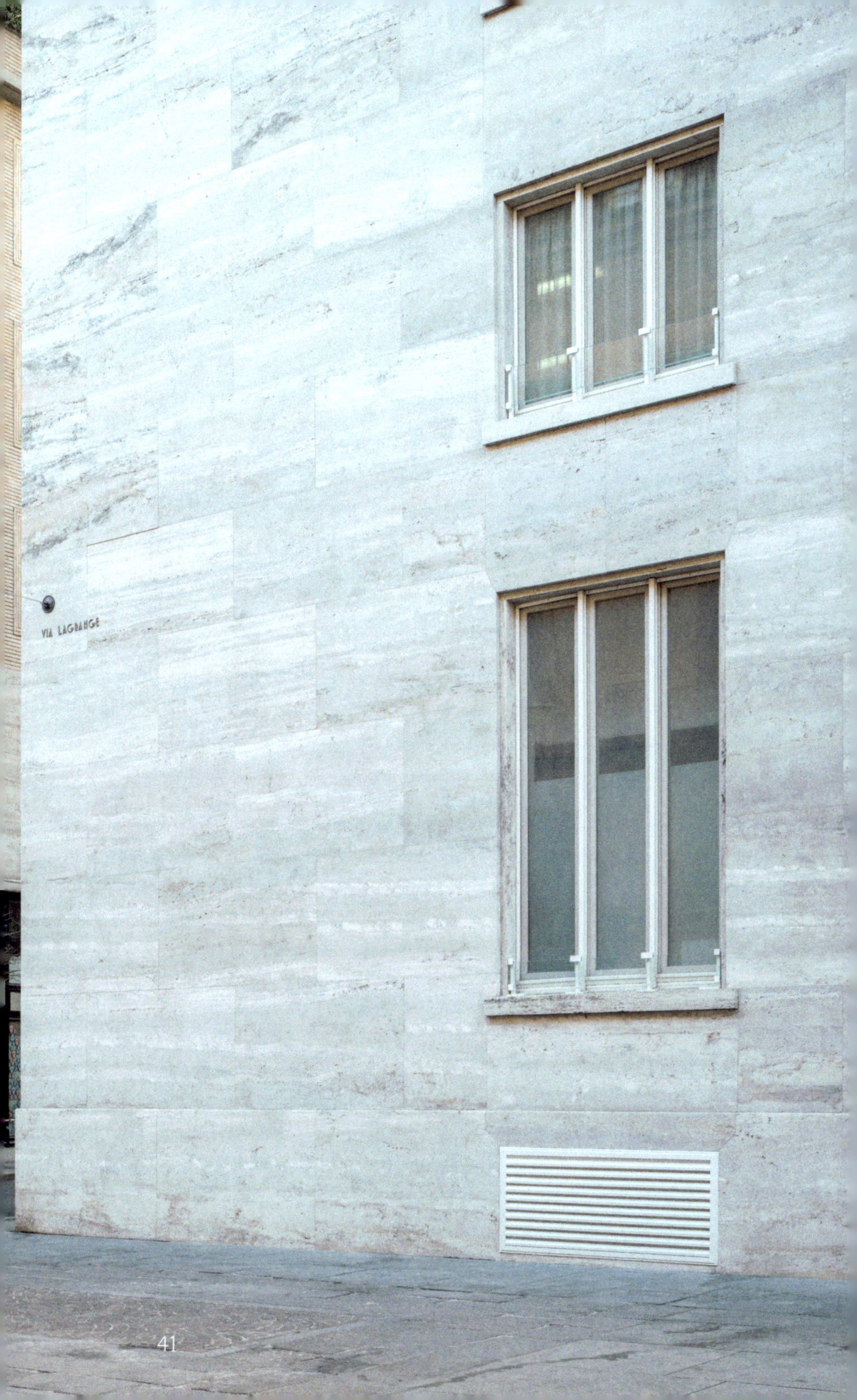
VIA LAGRANGE

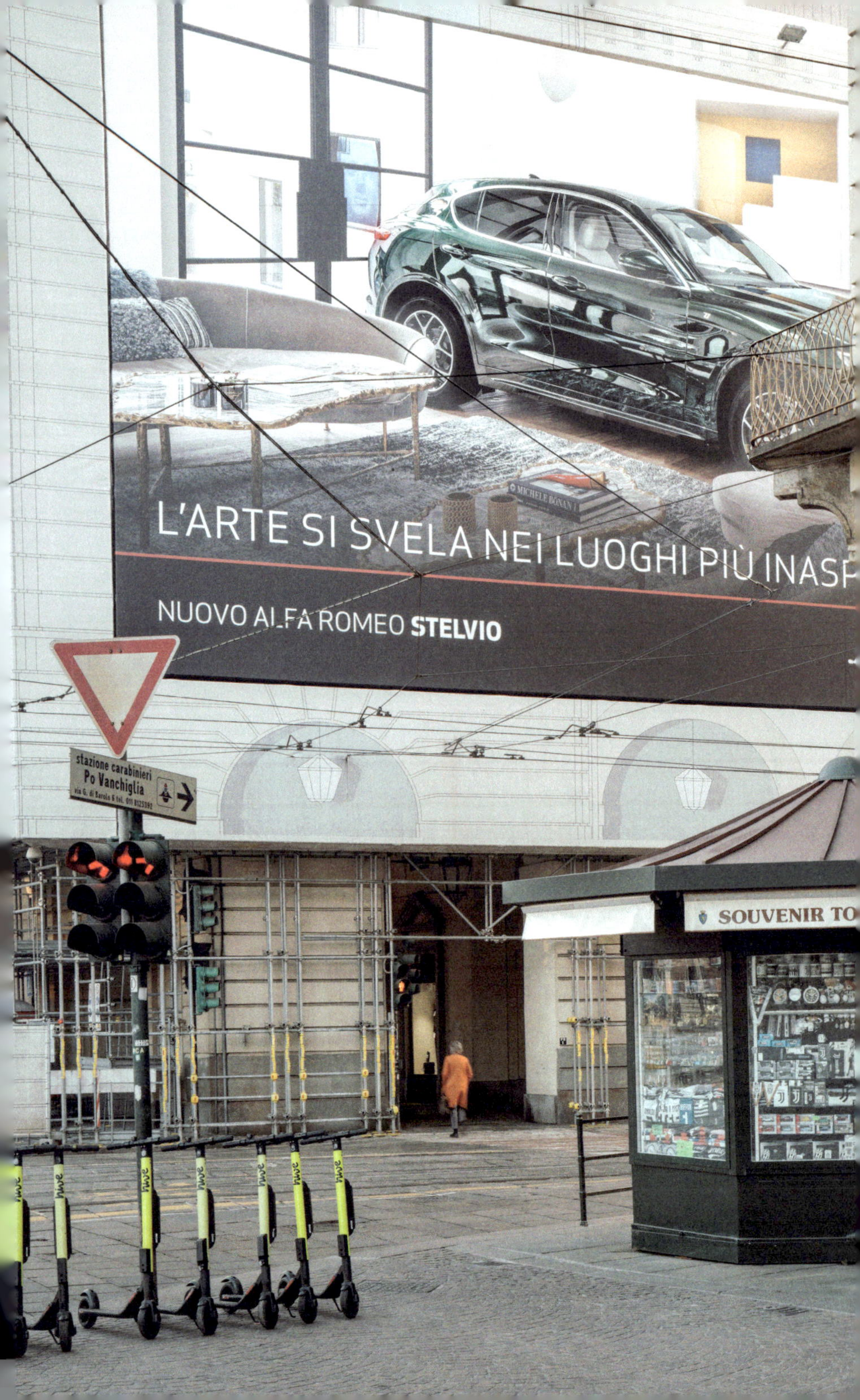
L'ARTE SI SVELA NEI LUOGHI PIÙ INASP
NUOVO ALFA ROMEO STELVIO
stazione carabinieri
Po Vanchiglia
SOUVENIR TO

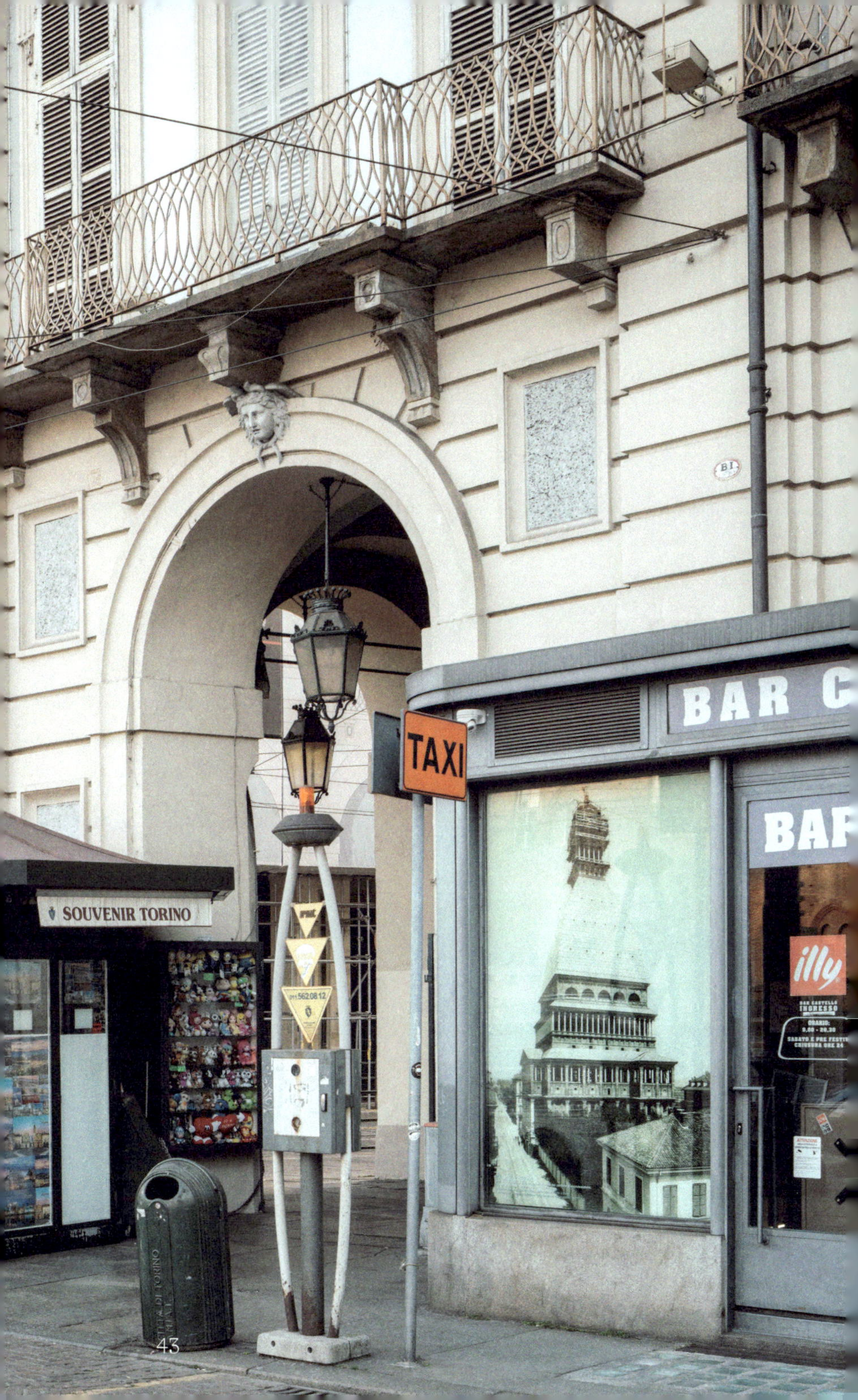
BAR C
TAXI
BAR
SOUVENIR TORINO
illy

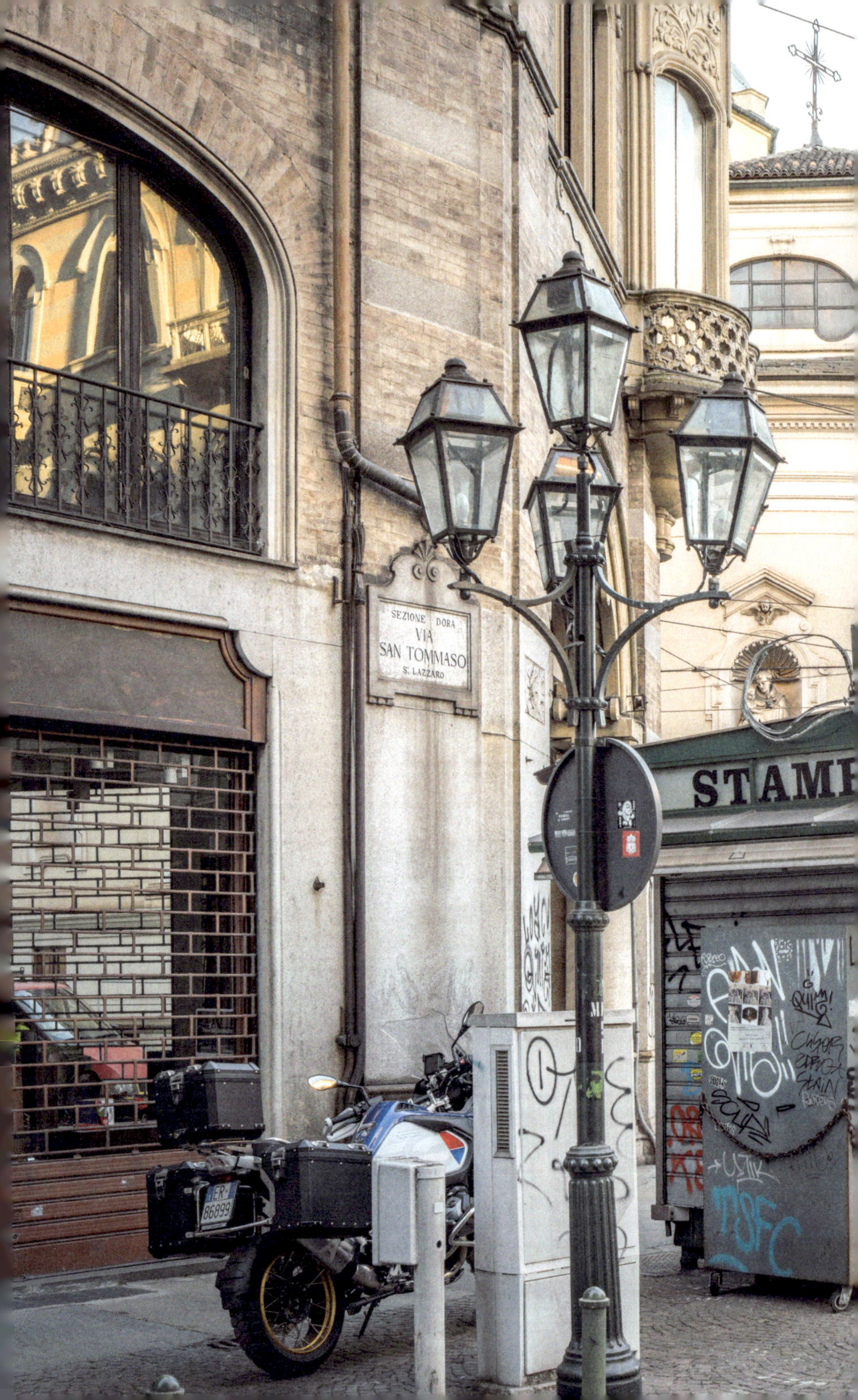
SEZIONE DORA
VIA
SAN TOMMASO
S. LAZZARO
STAM

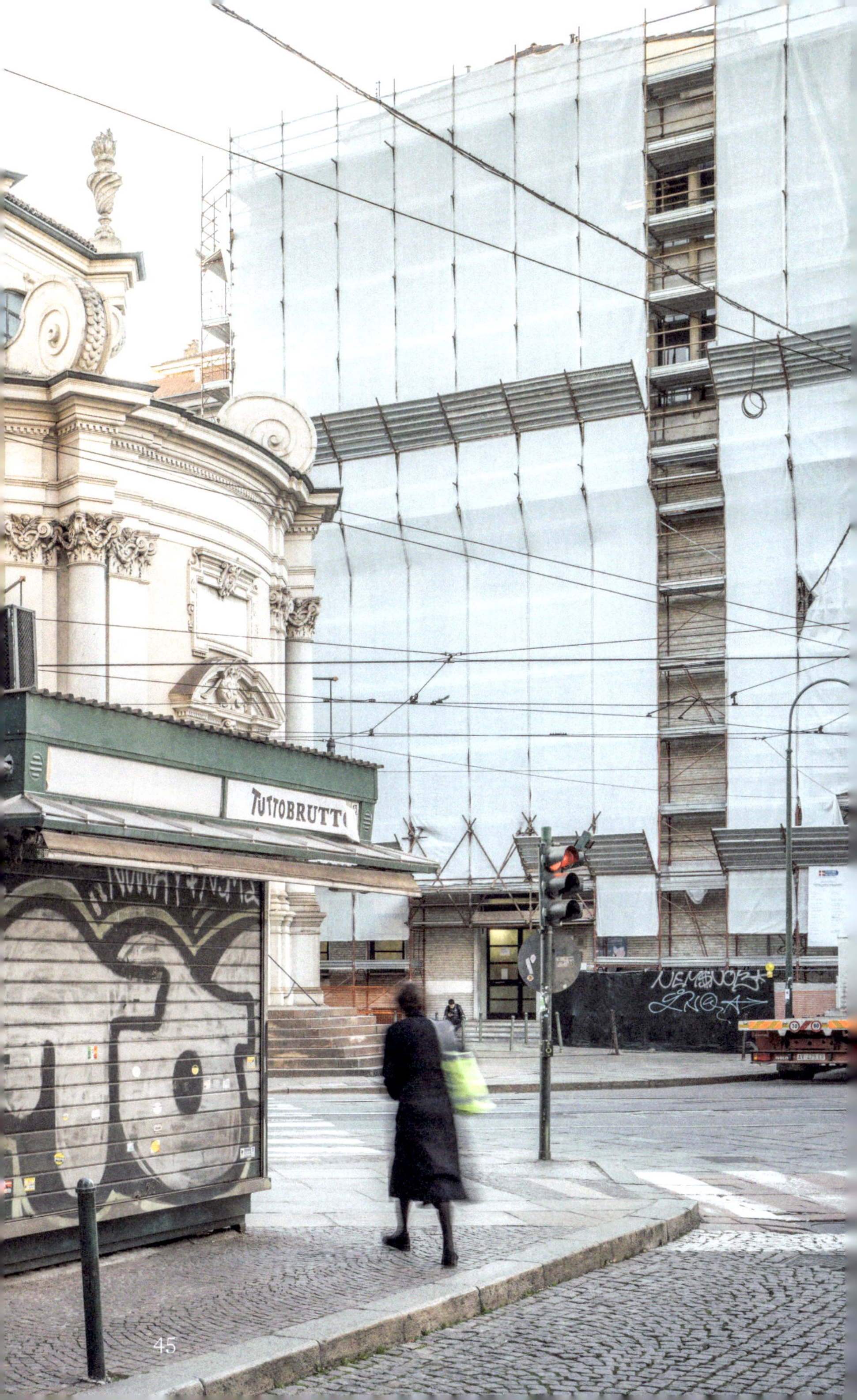
TUTTOBRUTT

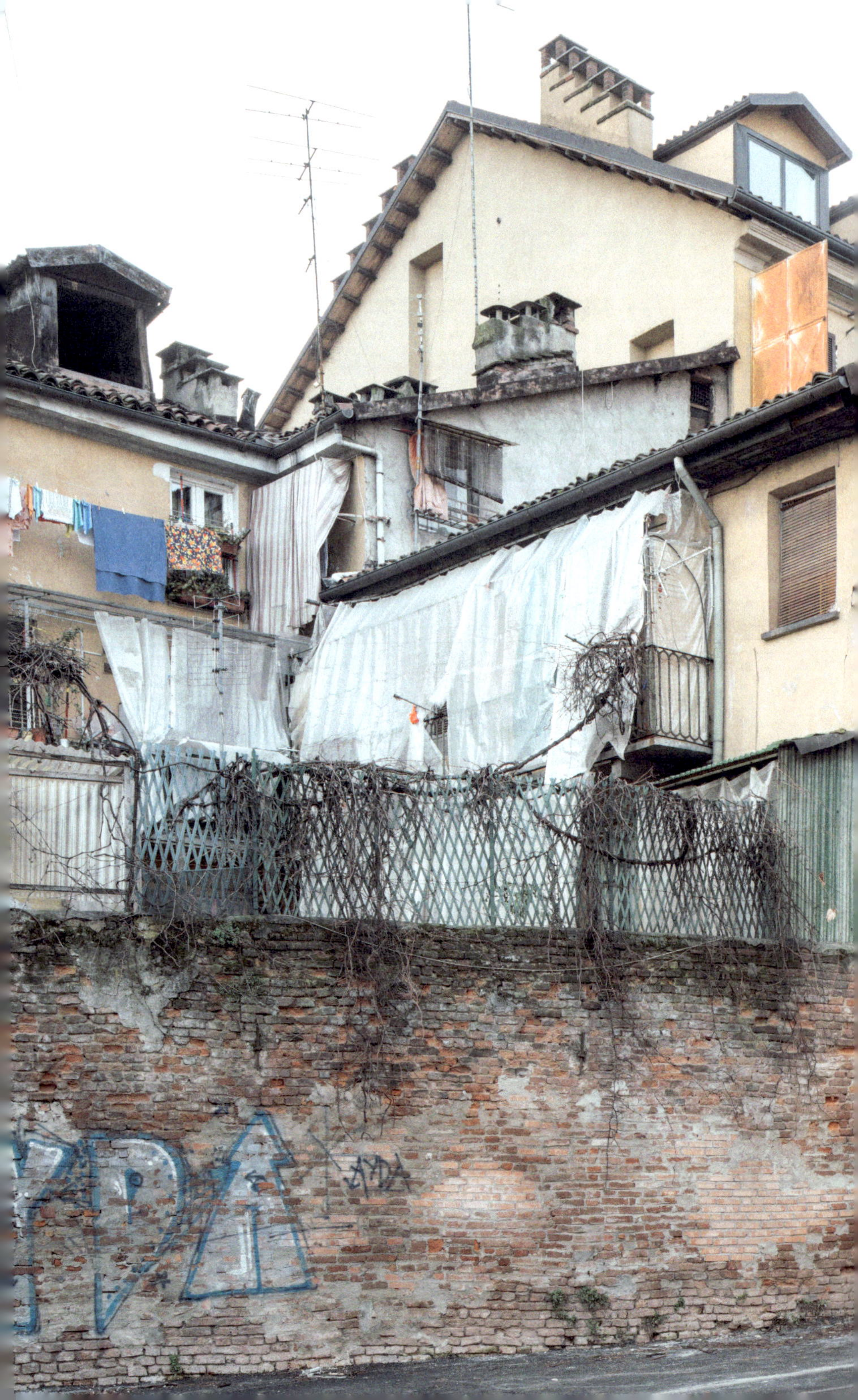

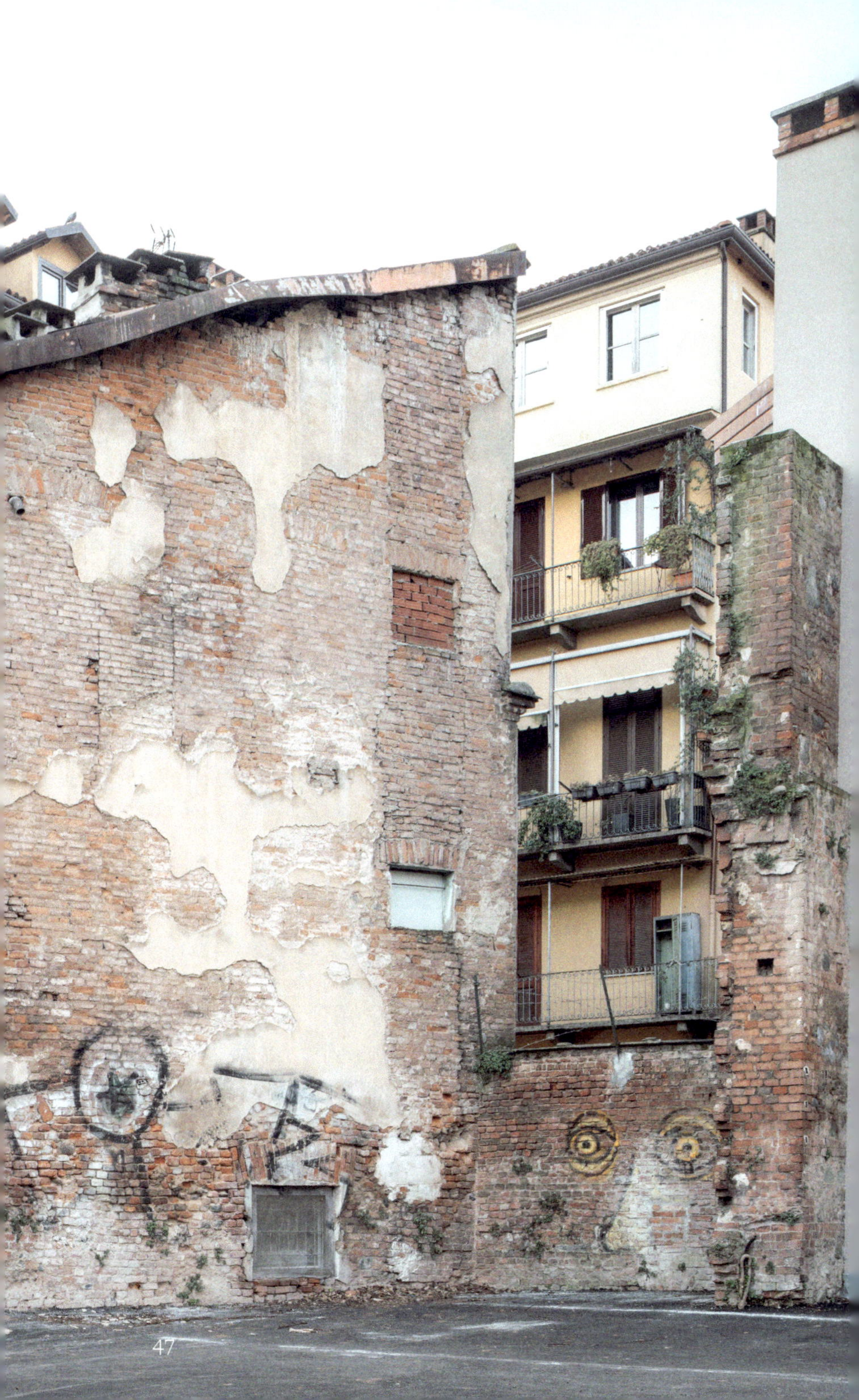

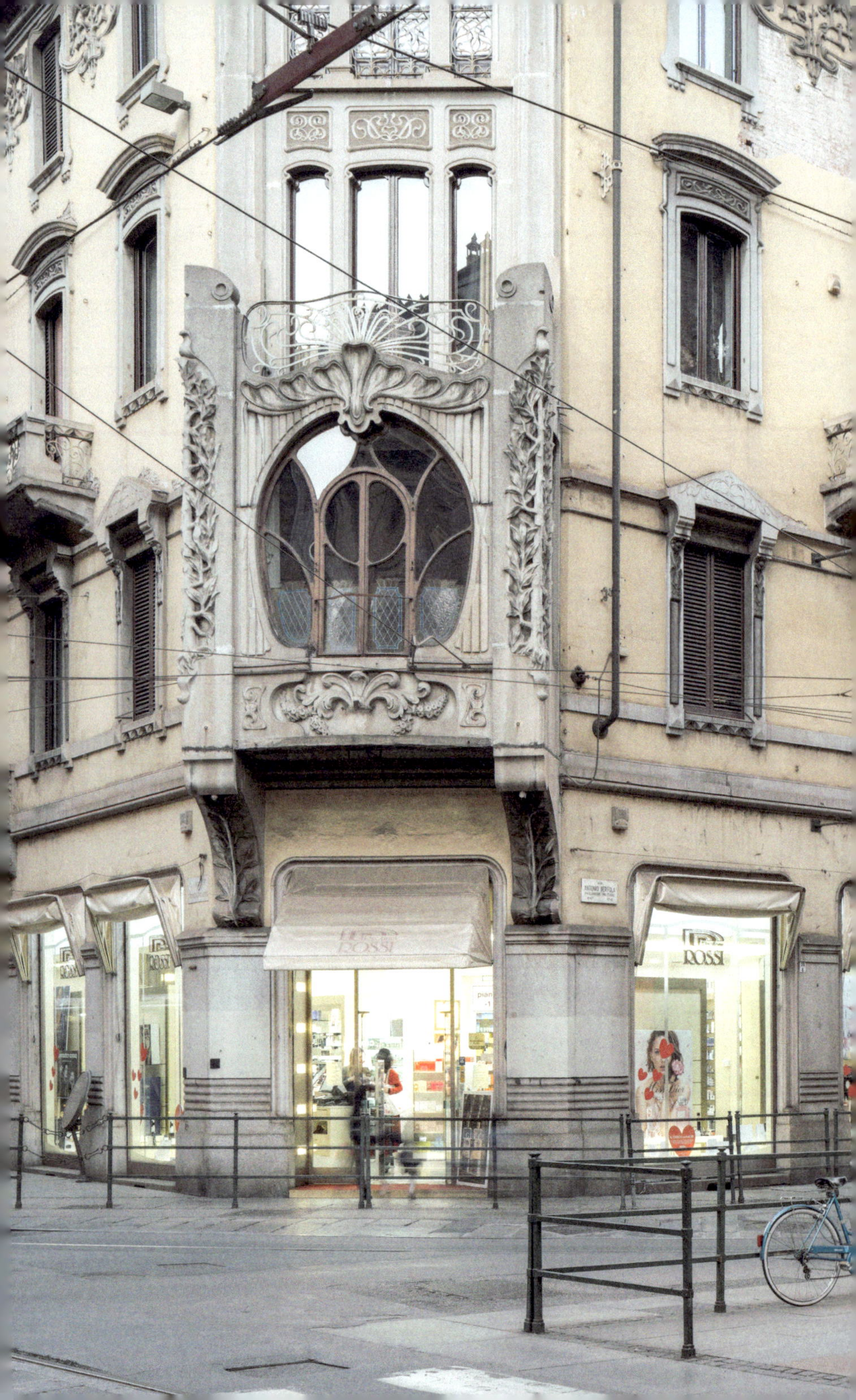
ROSSI
ANTONIO BERTOLA
ROSSI
ROSSI

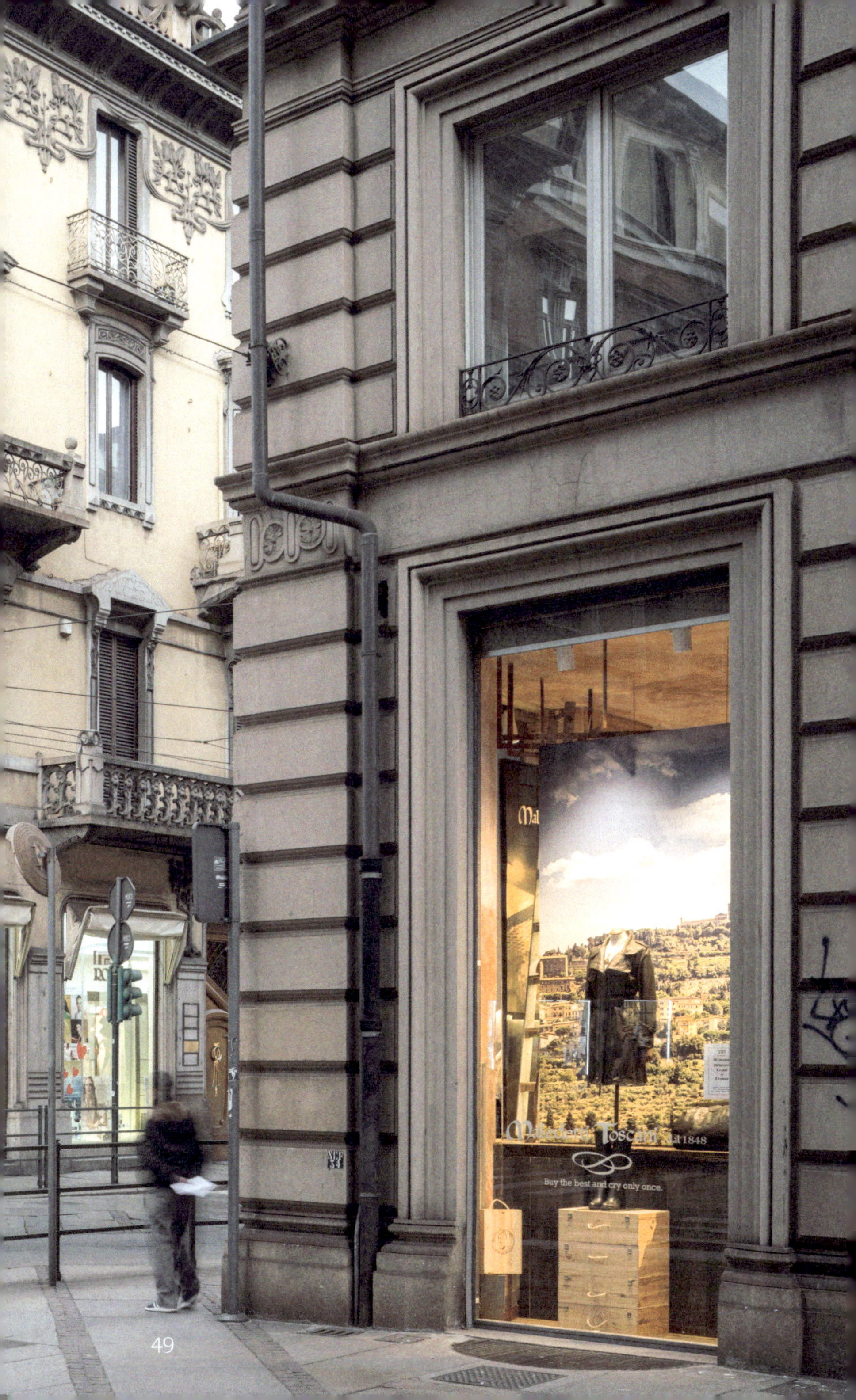
Maledetti Toscani dal 1848
Buy the best and cry only once.

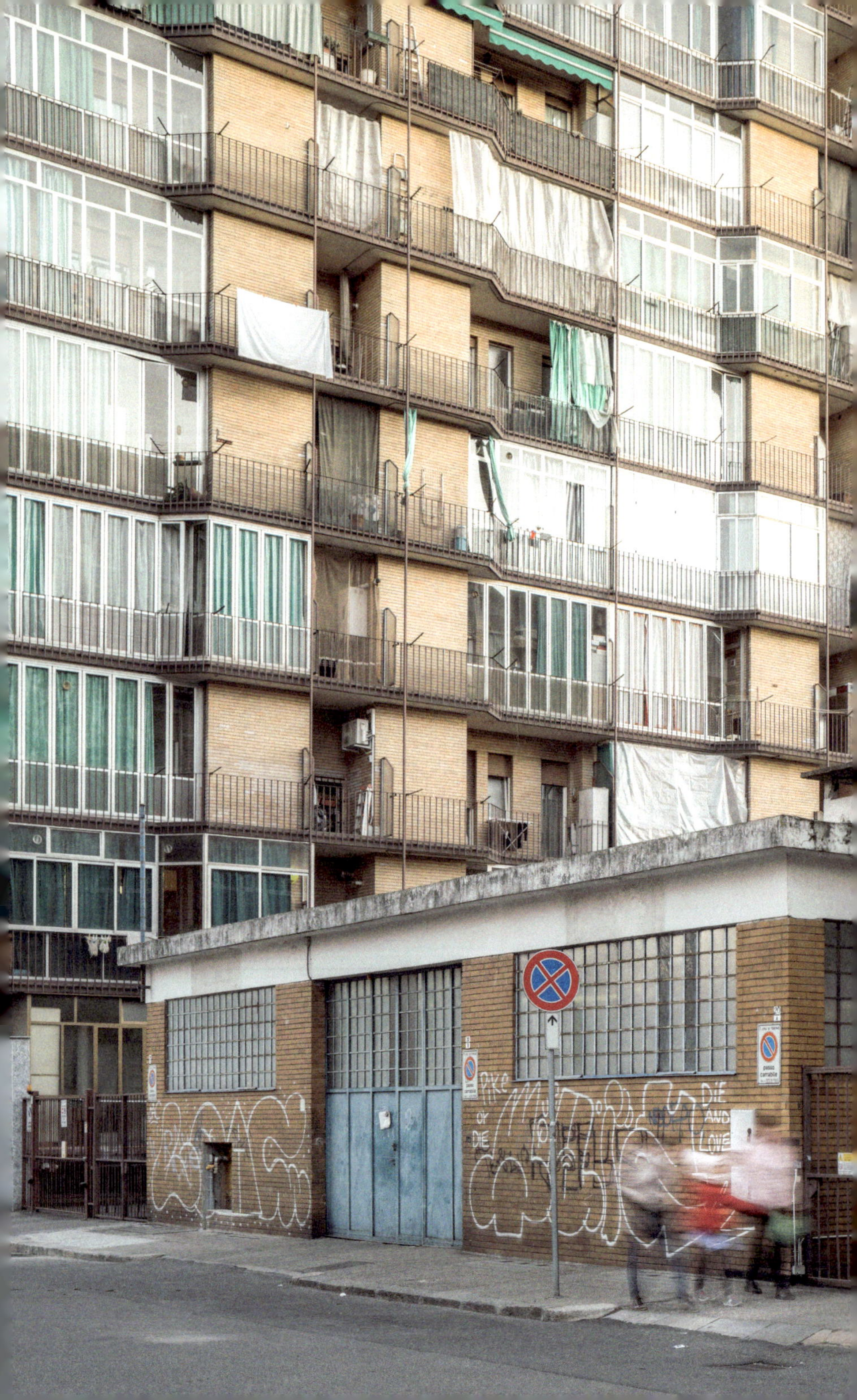
passo carrabile
PIKE OF DIE
DIE AND LOVE

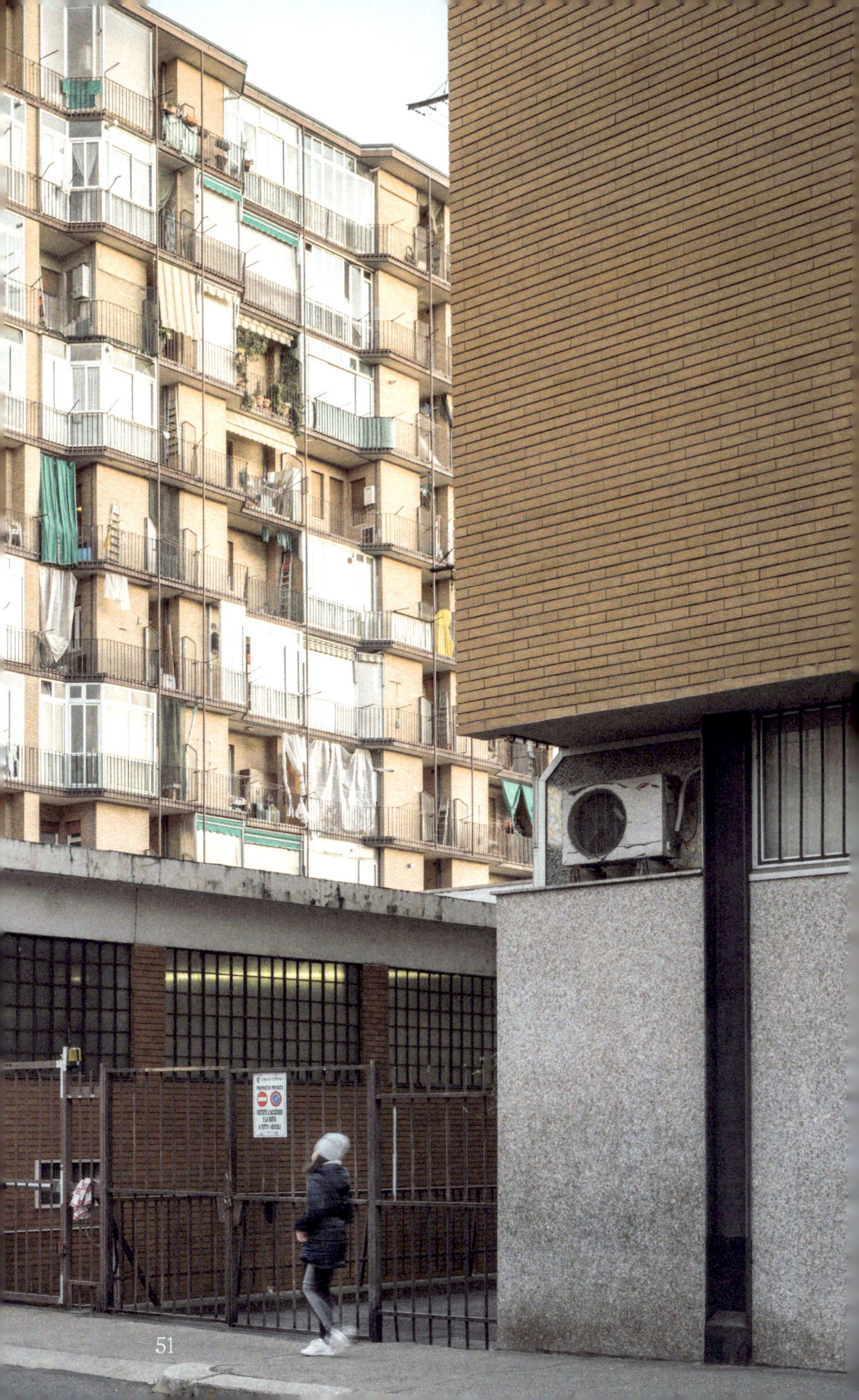
PROPRIETA' PRIVATA
VIETATO L'ACCESSO
E LA SOSTA
A TUTTI I VEICOLI

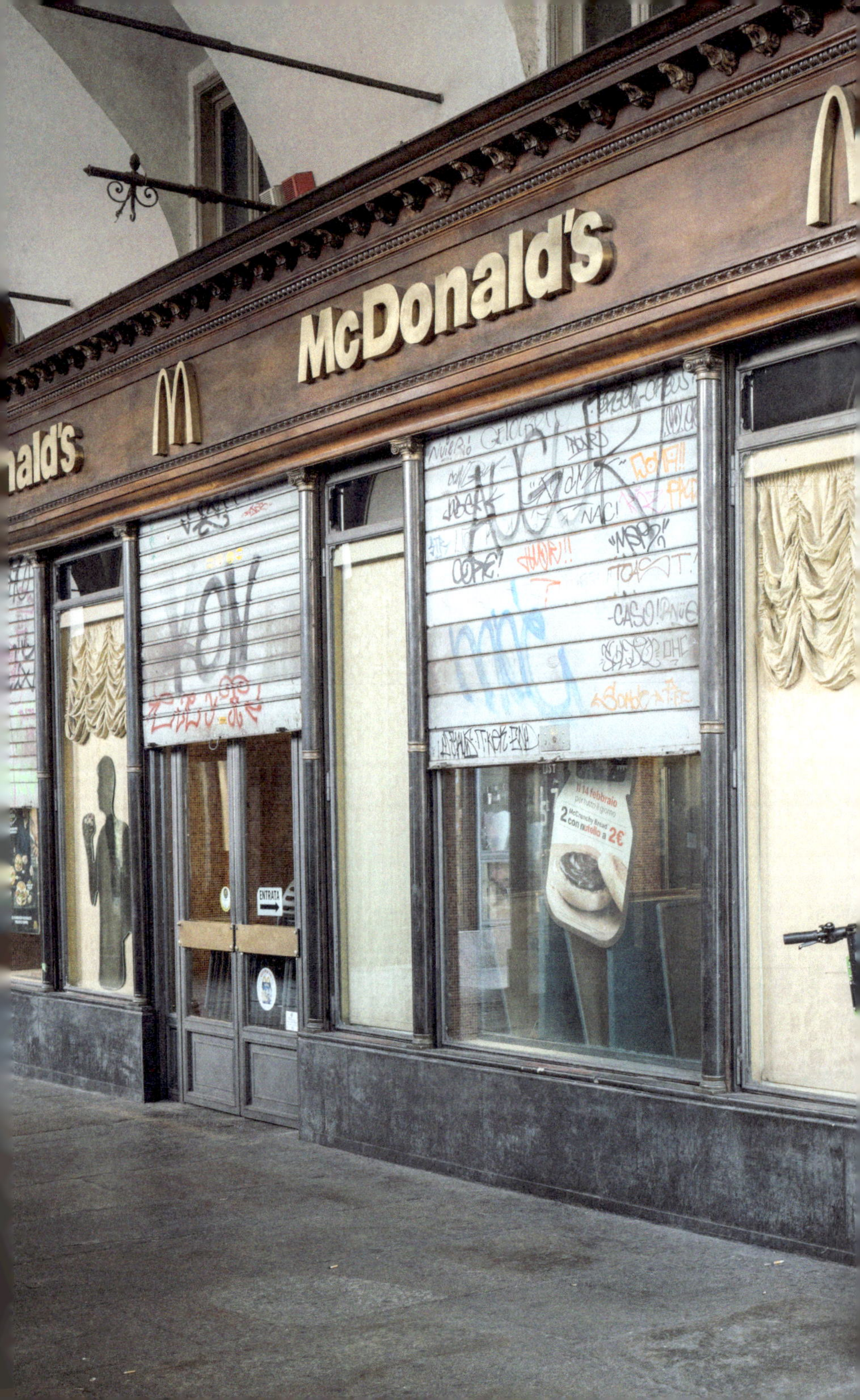
McDonald's
nald's
ENTRATA
Il 14 febbraio
per tutto il giorno
2 McCrunchy Bread con nutella a 2€

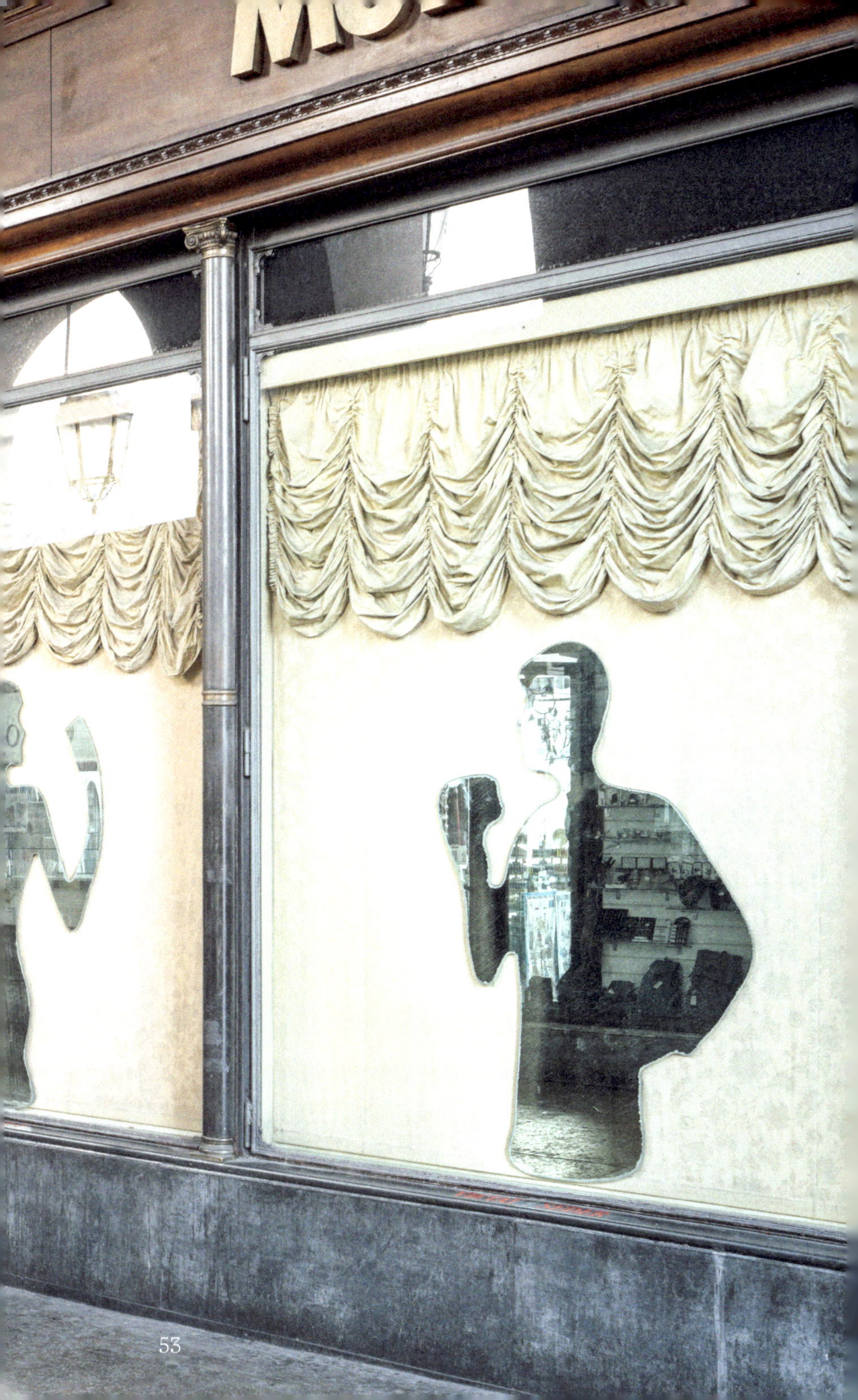

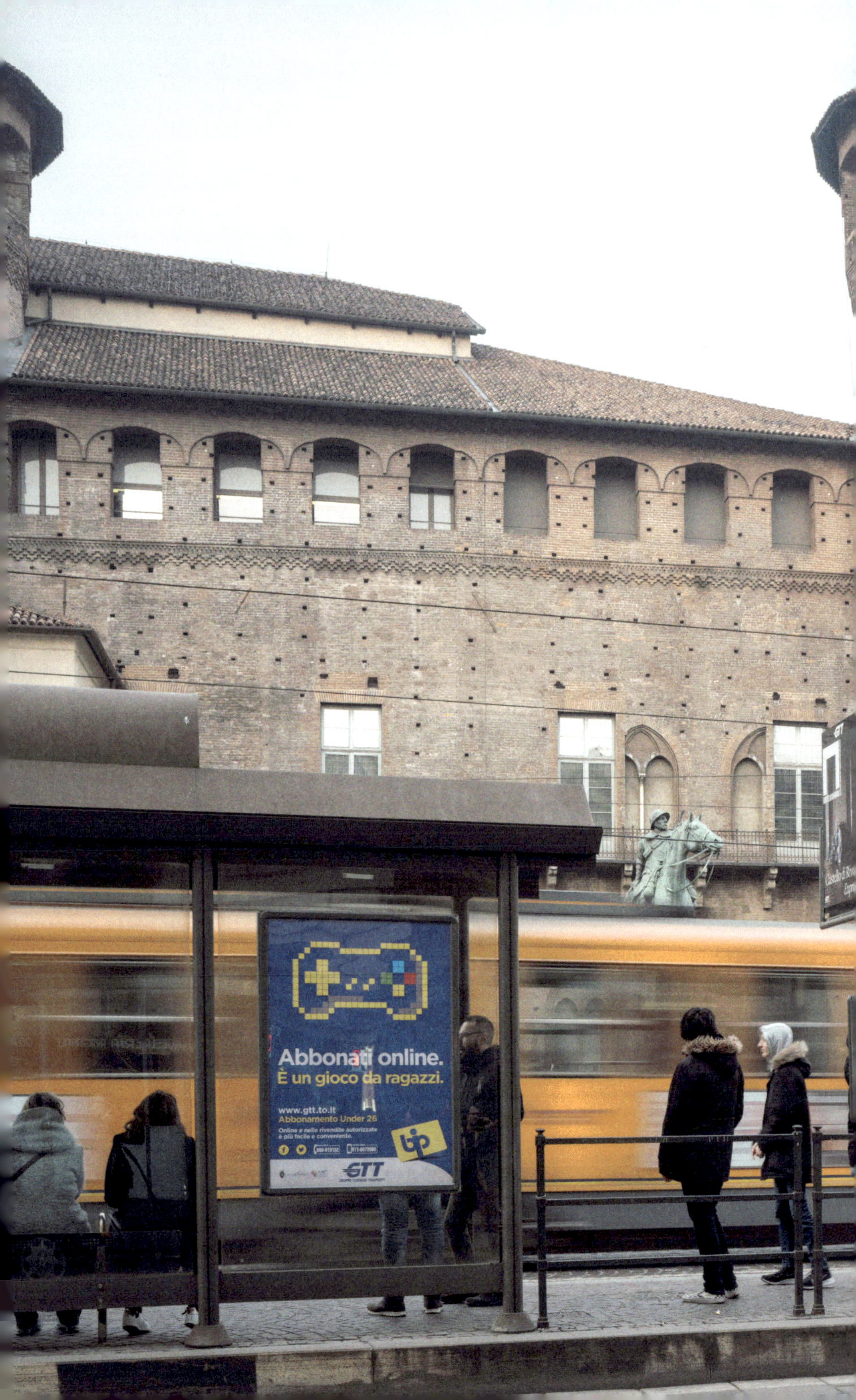
Abbonati online.
È un gioco da ragazzi.
www.gtt.to.it
Abbonamento Under 26
Online e nelle rivendite autorizzate è più facile e conveniente.
GTT

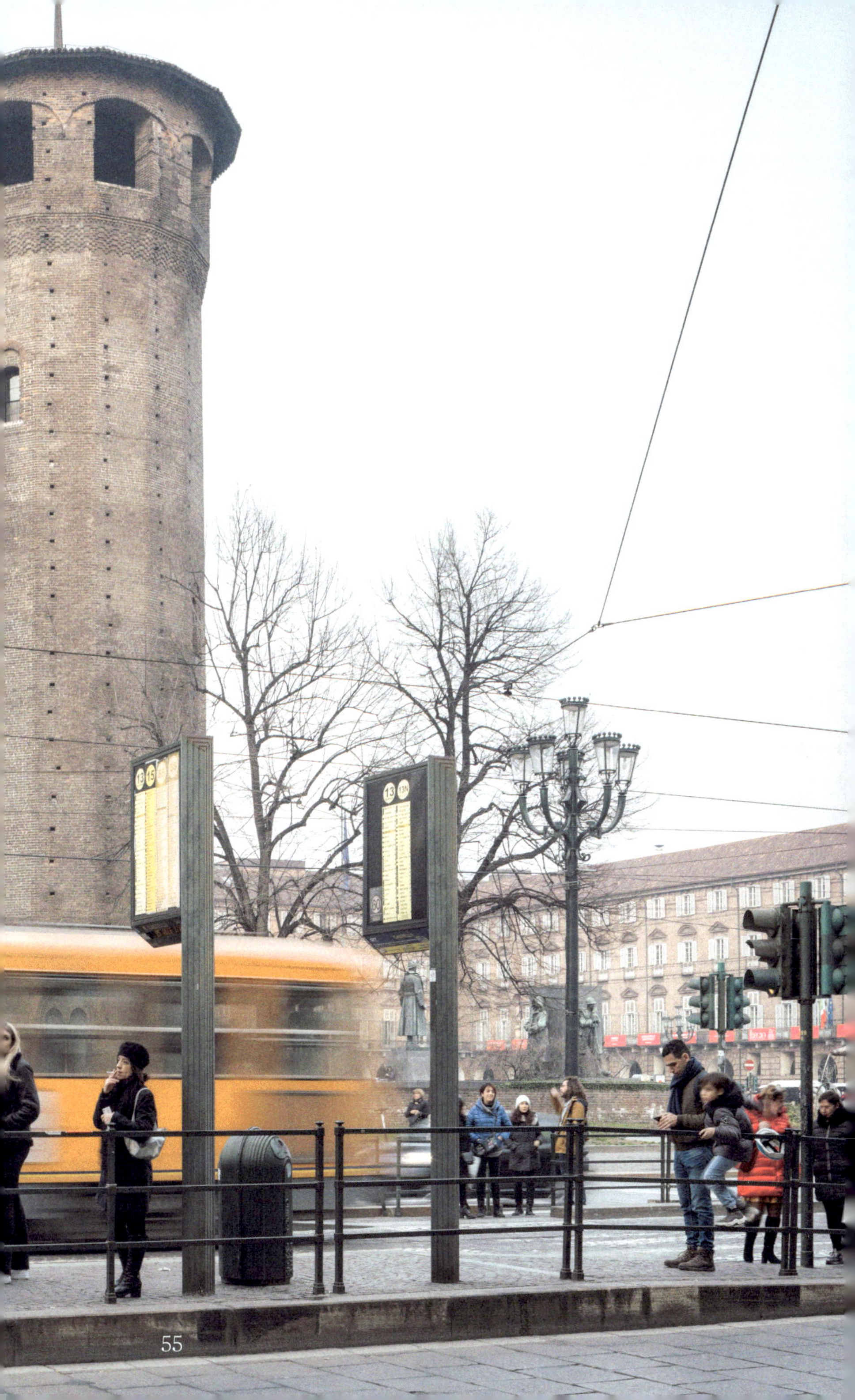

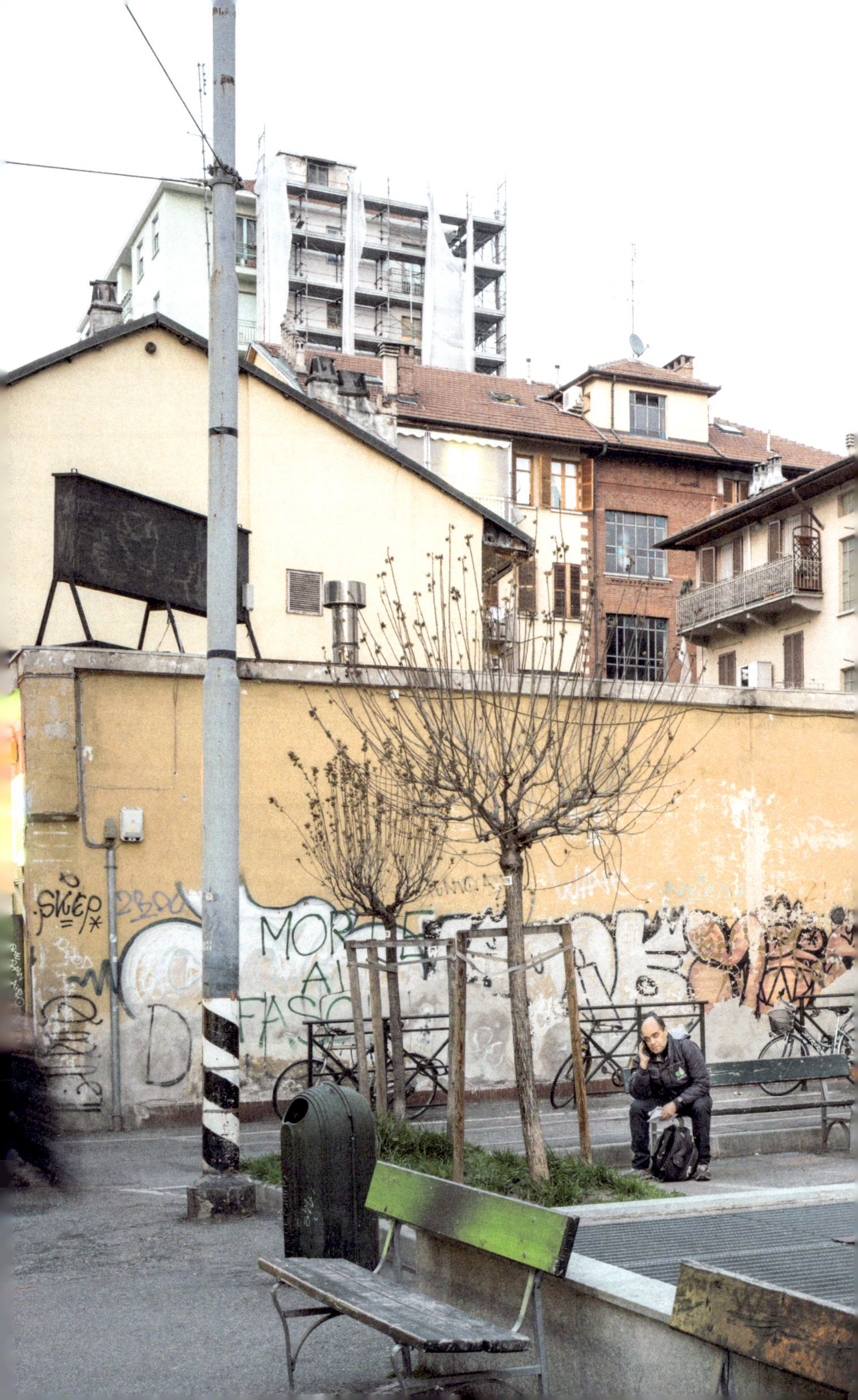
MORTE
AI

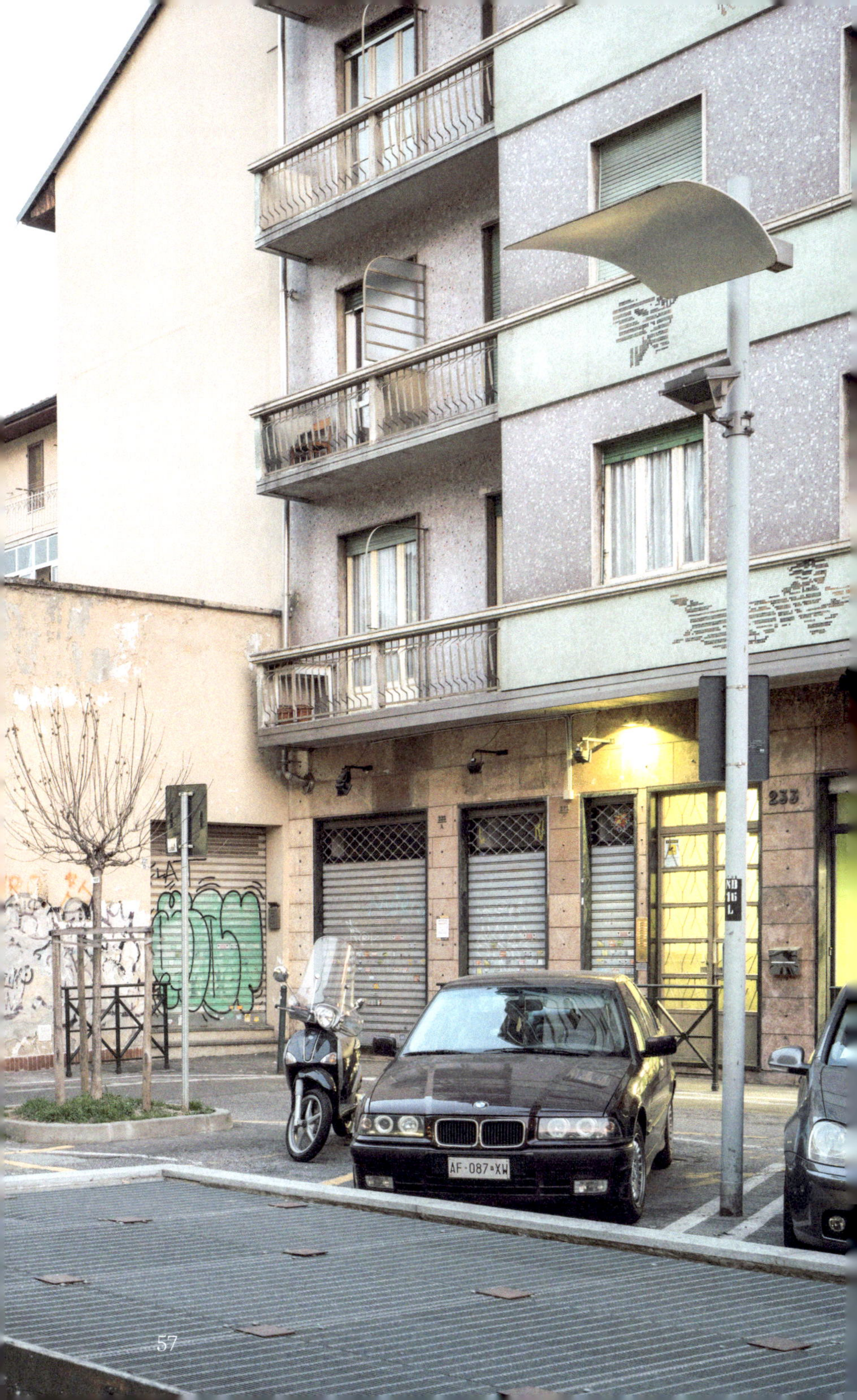
233
AF·087·XW

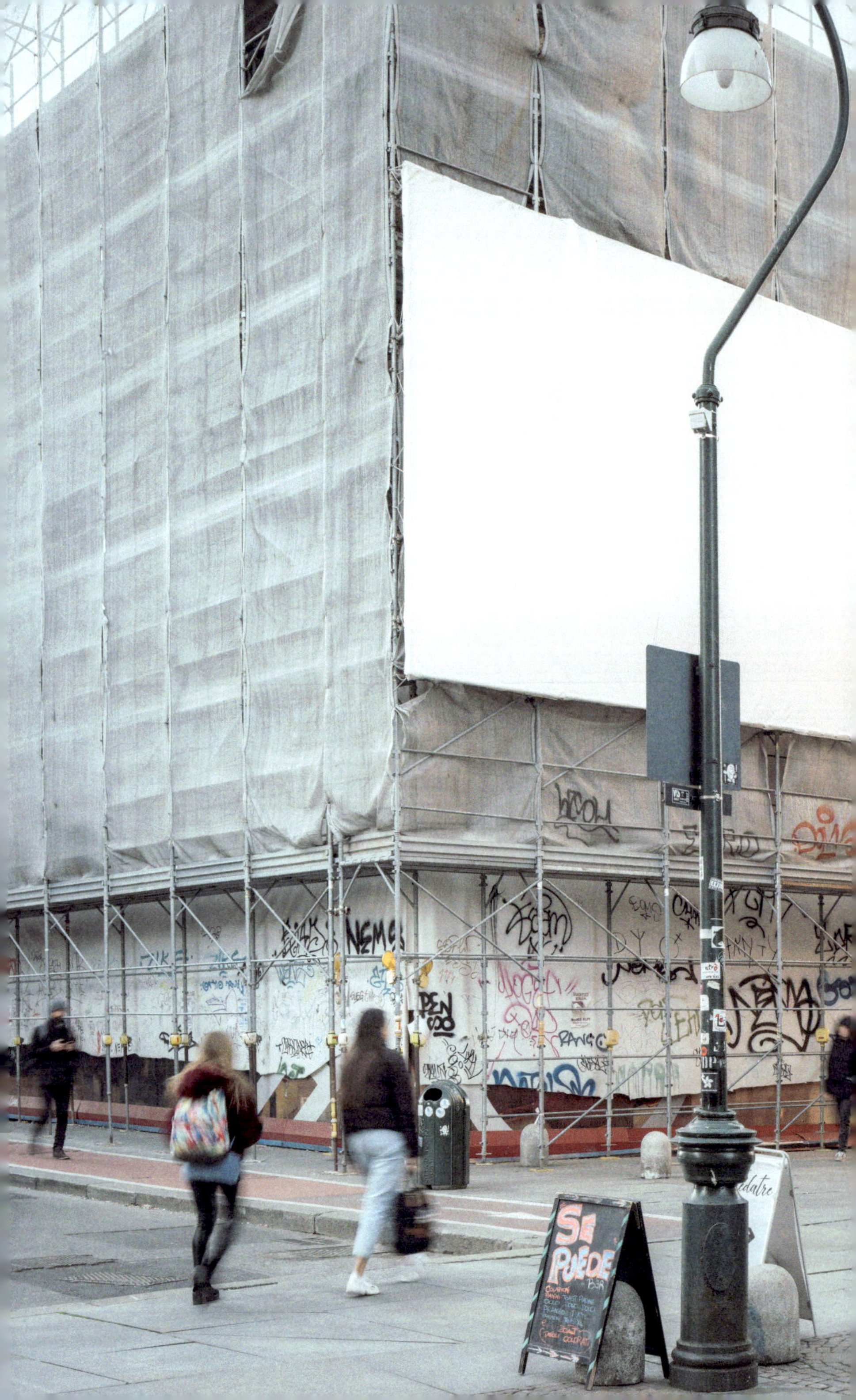
SE PUEDE

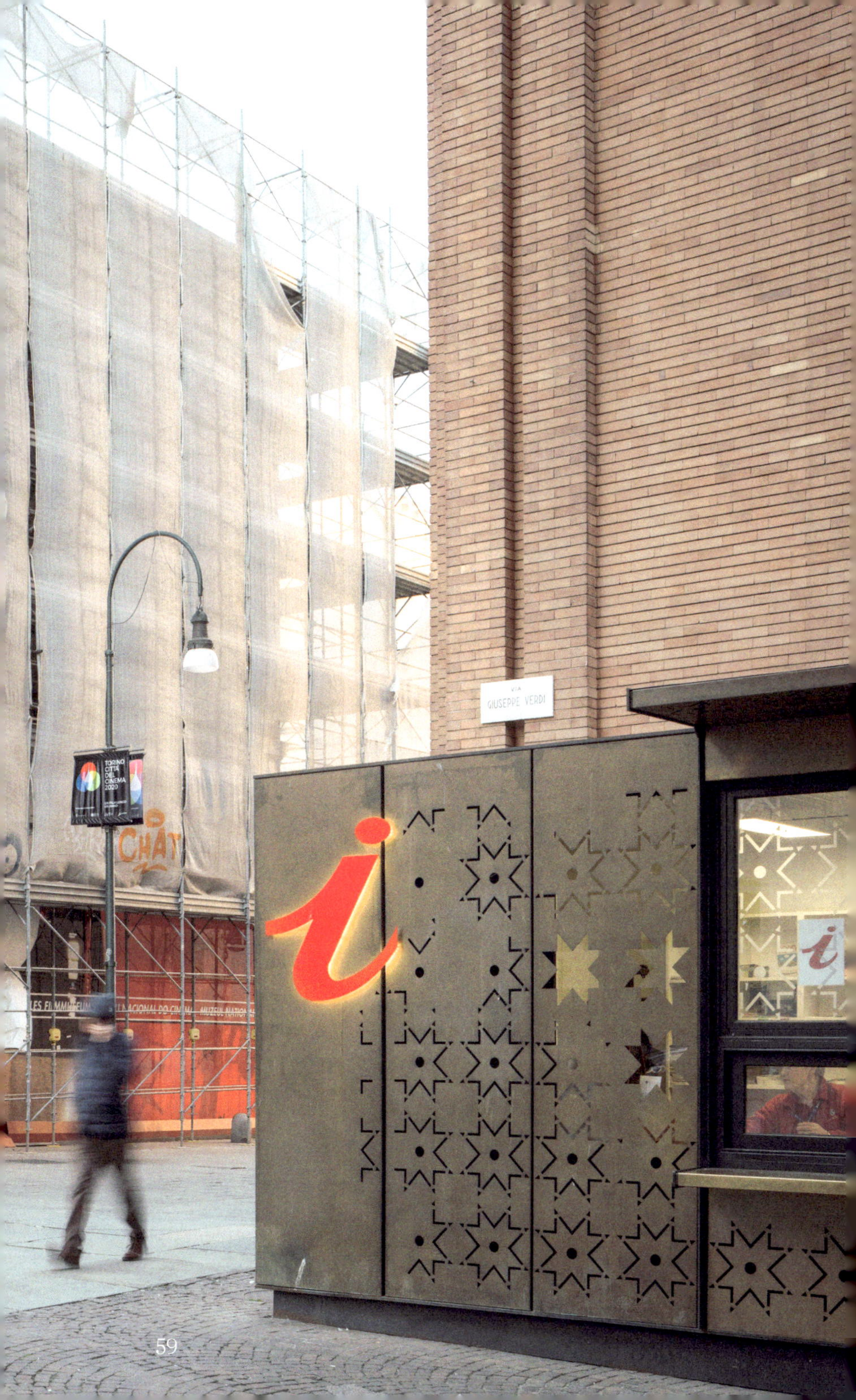
TORINO
CITTÀ
DEL
CINEMA
2020
VIA
GIUSEPPE VERDI

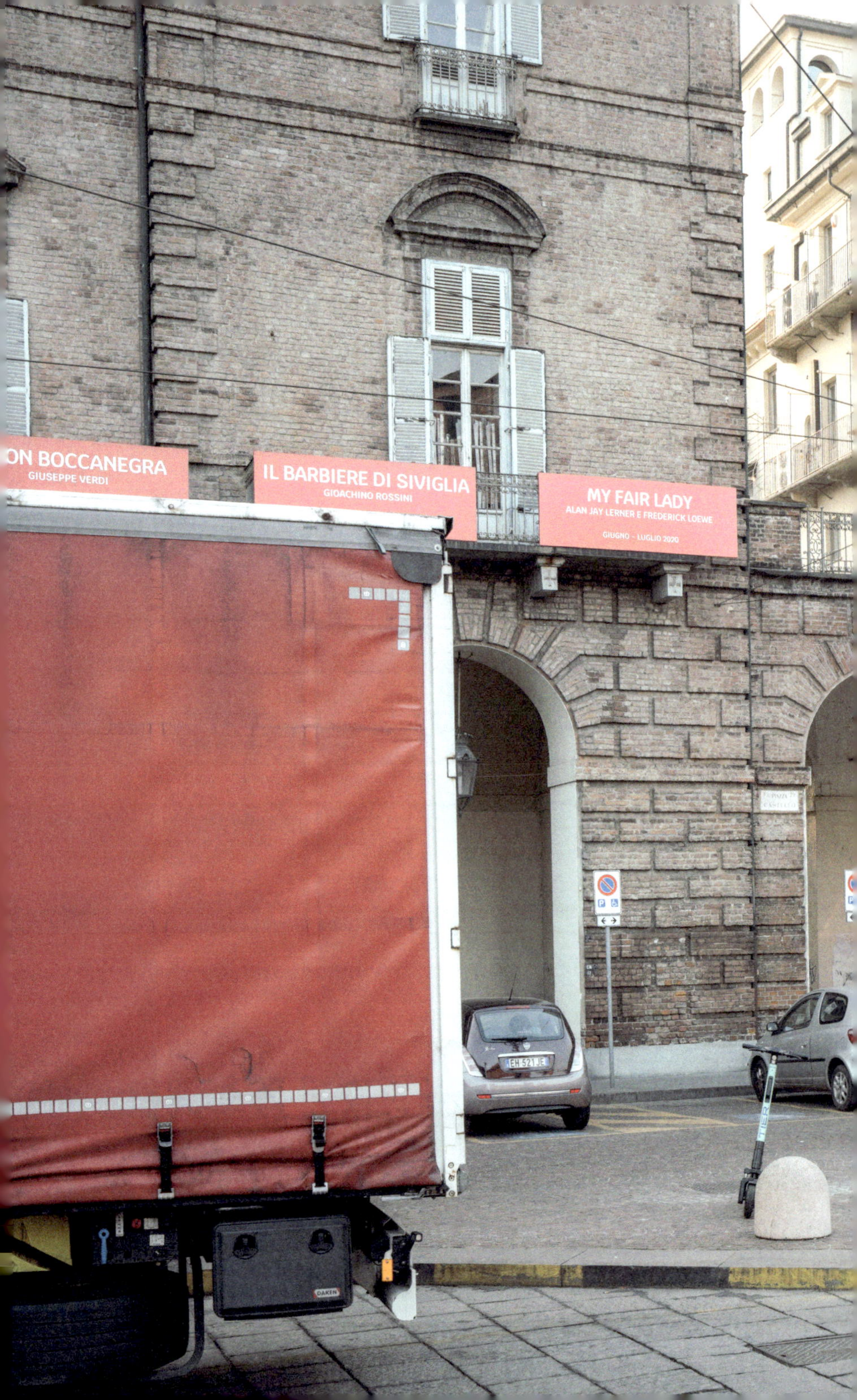
ON BOCCANEGRA
GIUSEPPE VERDI
IL BARBIERE DI SIVIGLIA
GIOACHINO ROSSINI
MY FAIR LADY
ALAN JAY LERNER E FREDERICK LOEWE
GIUGNO - LUGLIO 2020
EH 521 JE

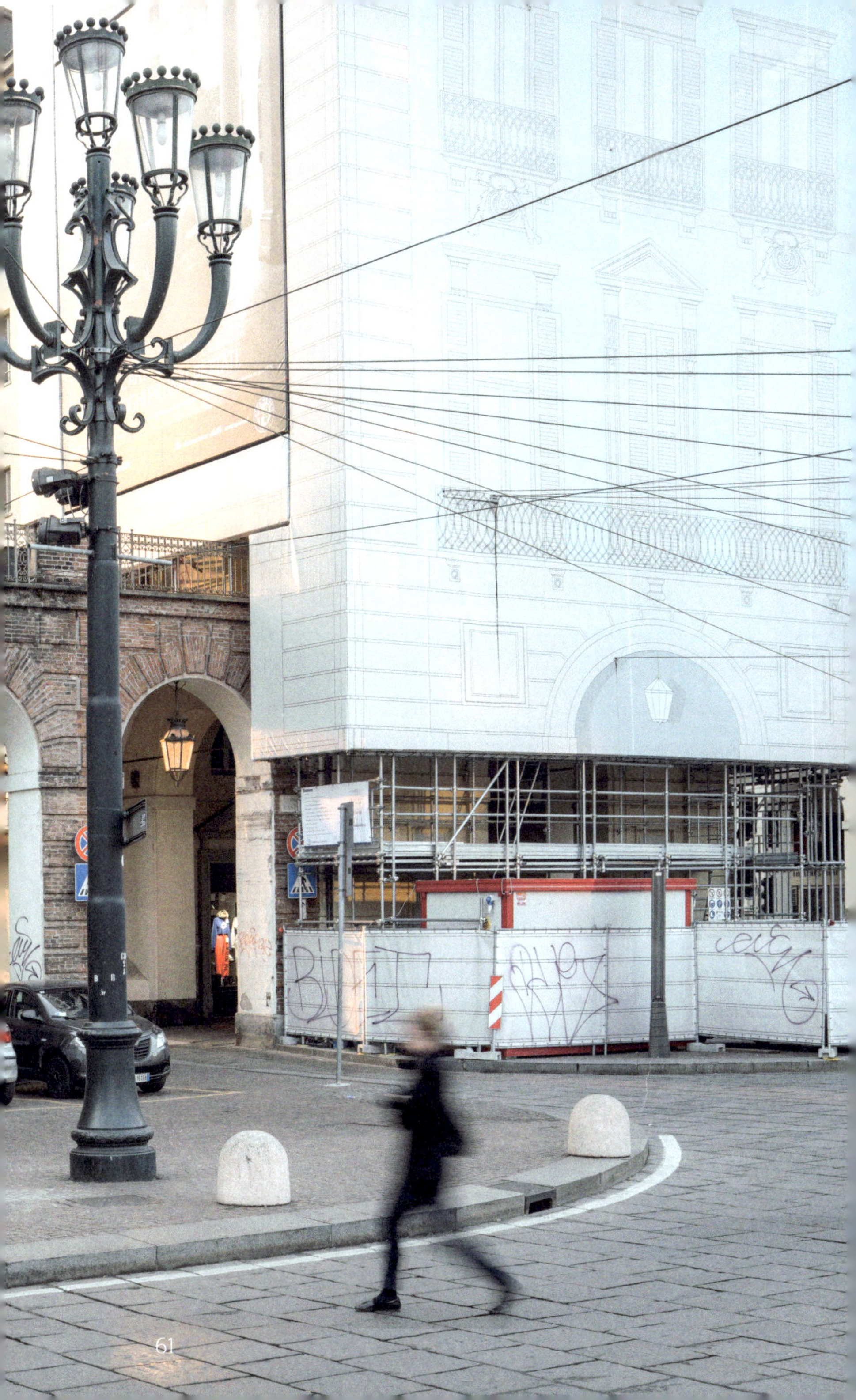

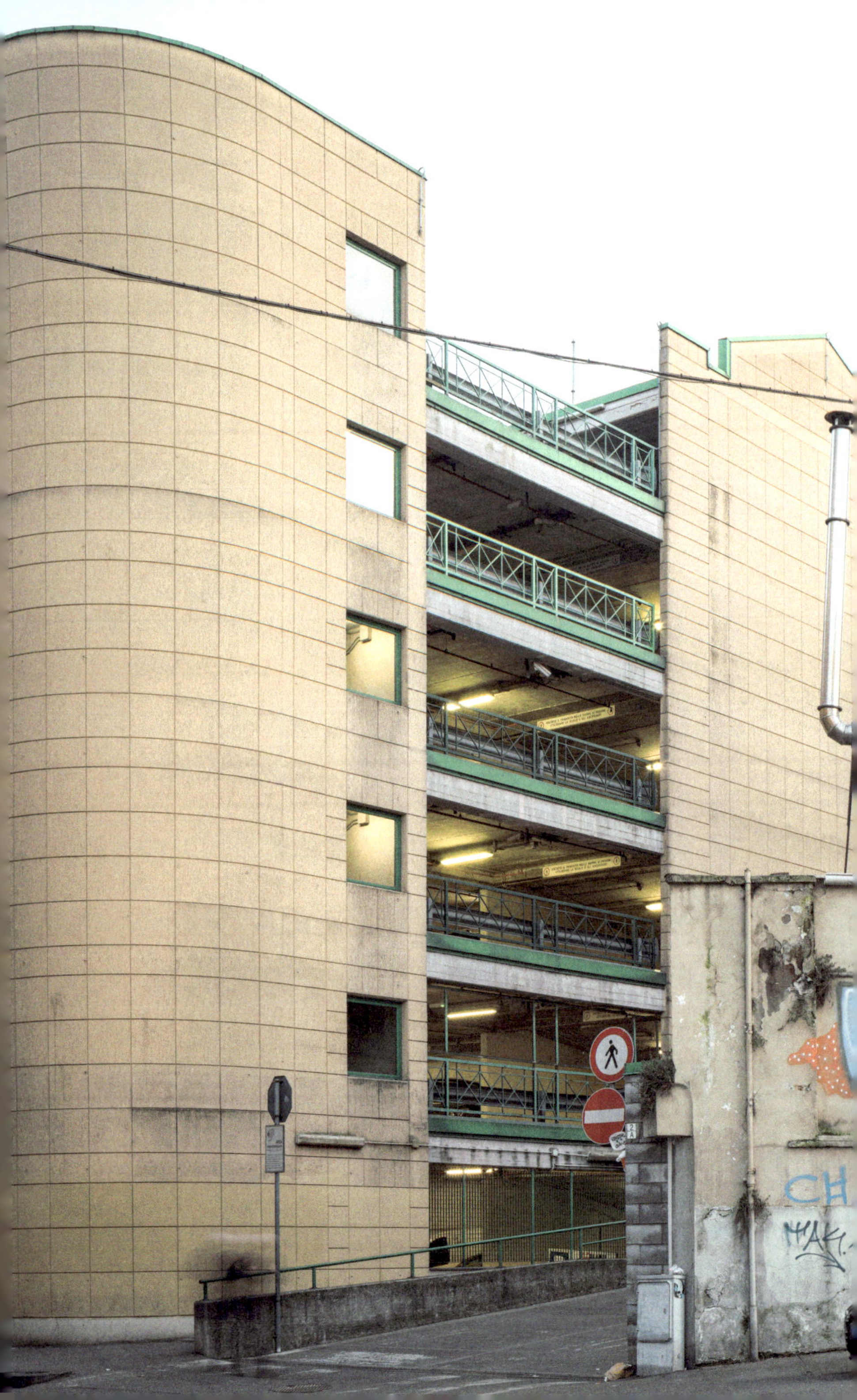

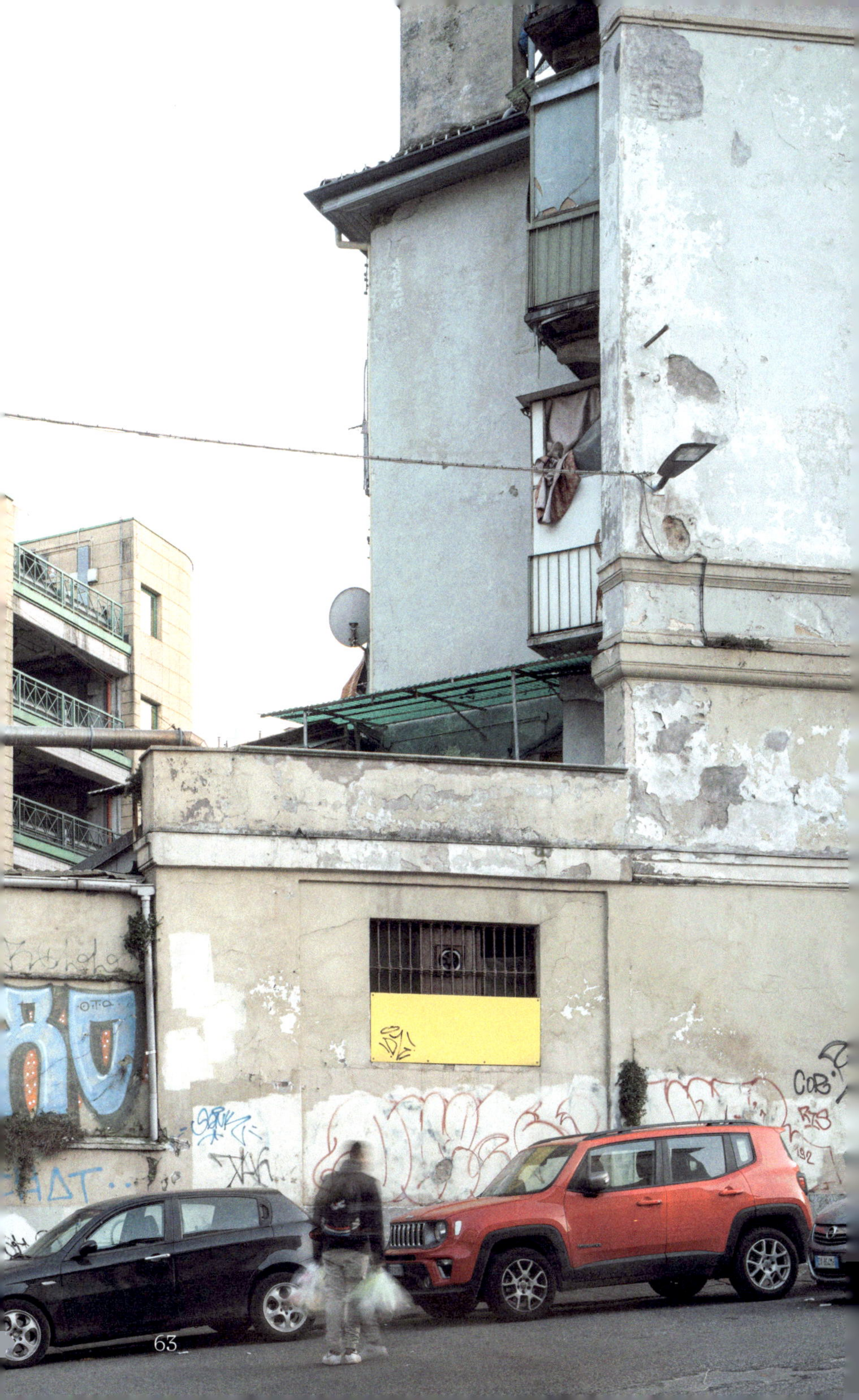

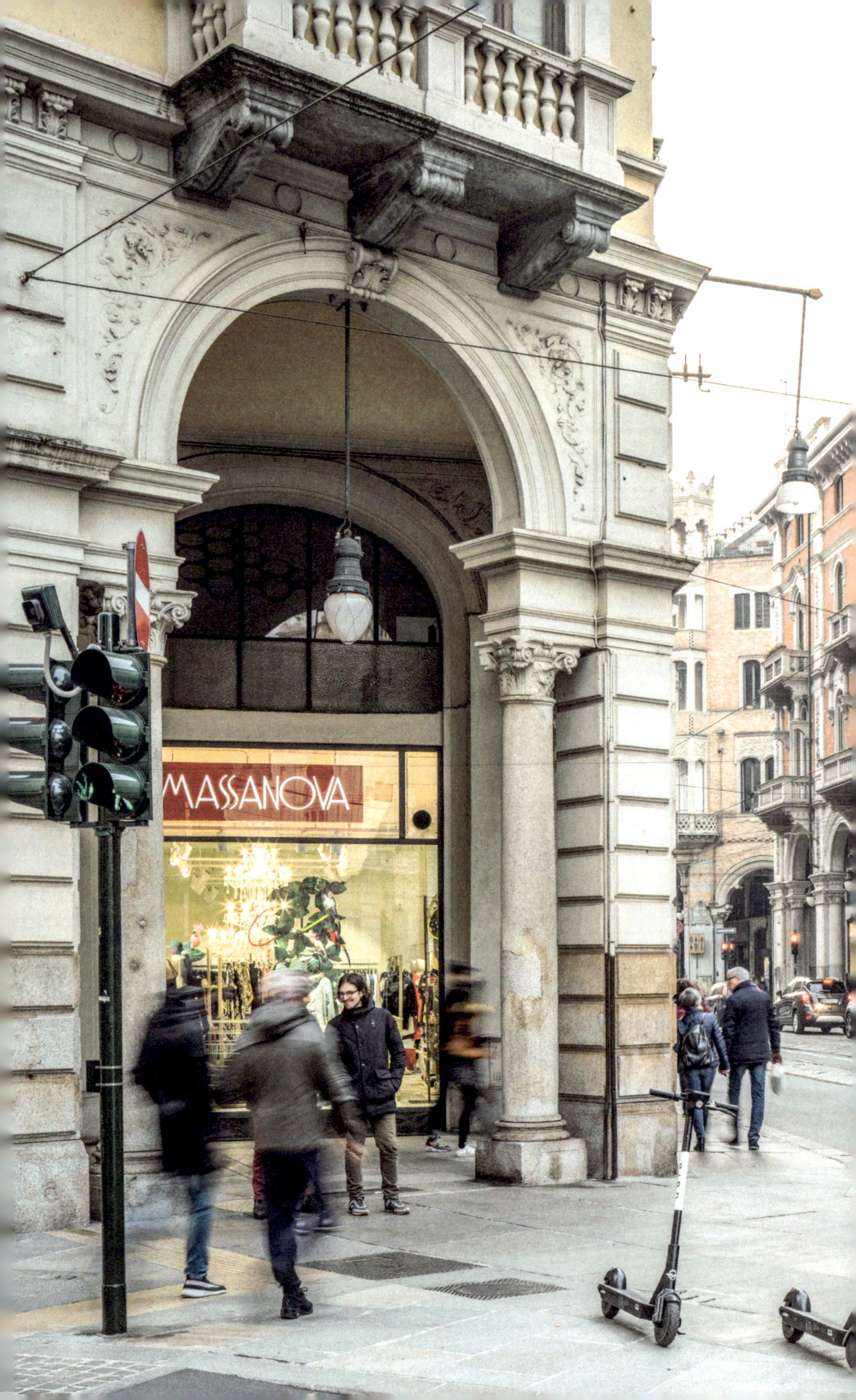
MASSANOVA

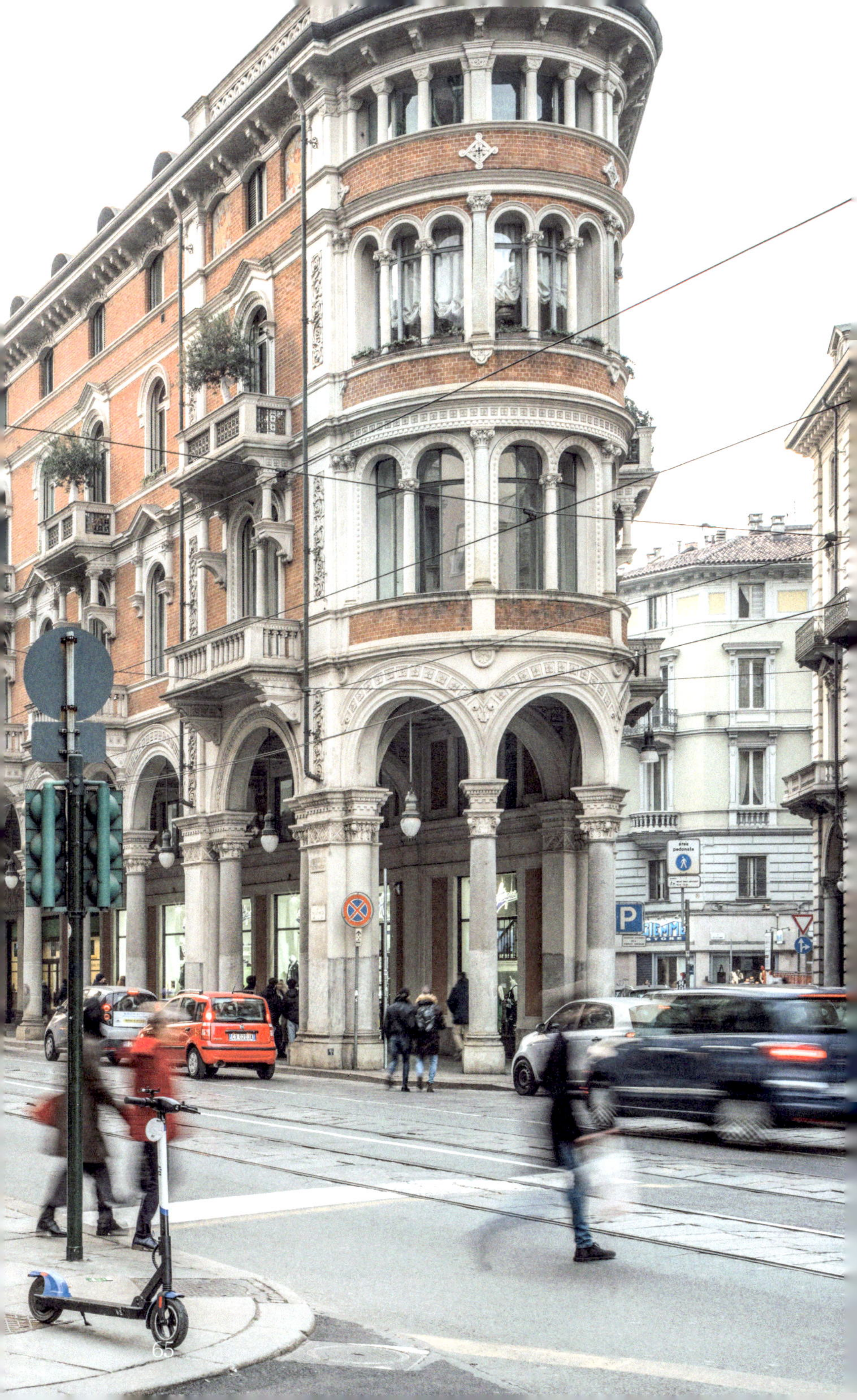

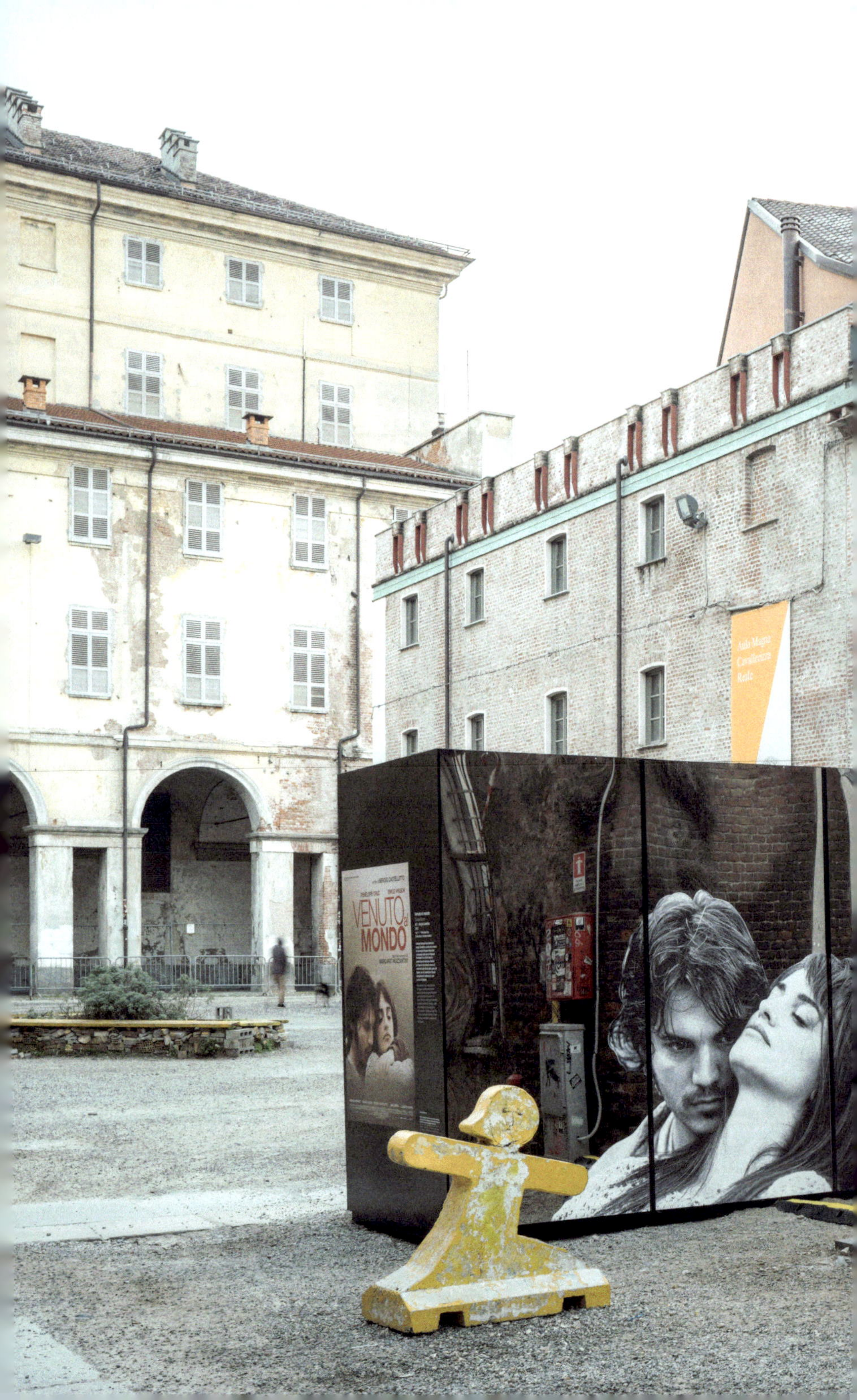
Aula Magna
Cavallerizza
Reale
VENUTO al MONDO

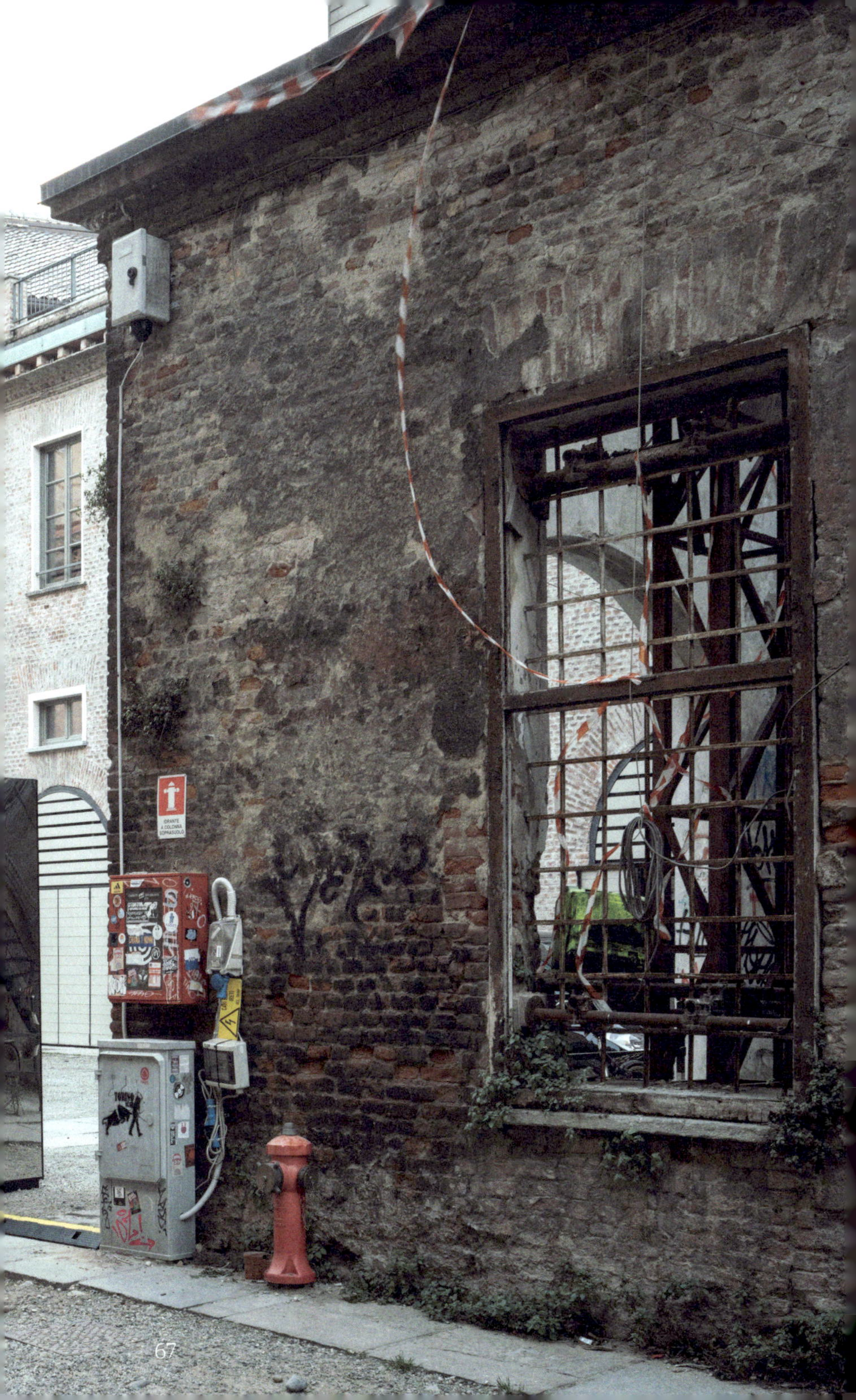
IDRANTE
A COLONNA
SOPRASUOLO

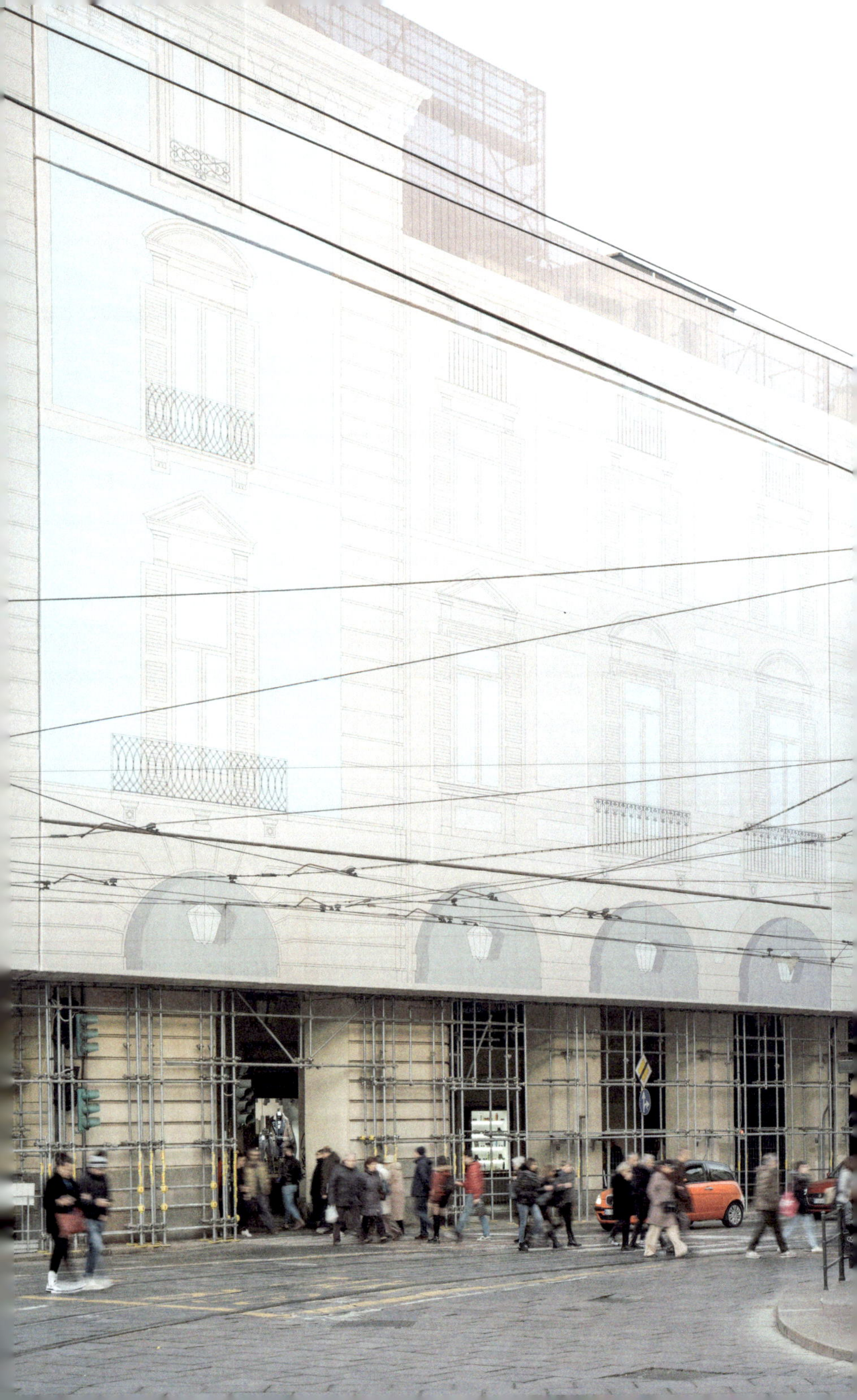

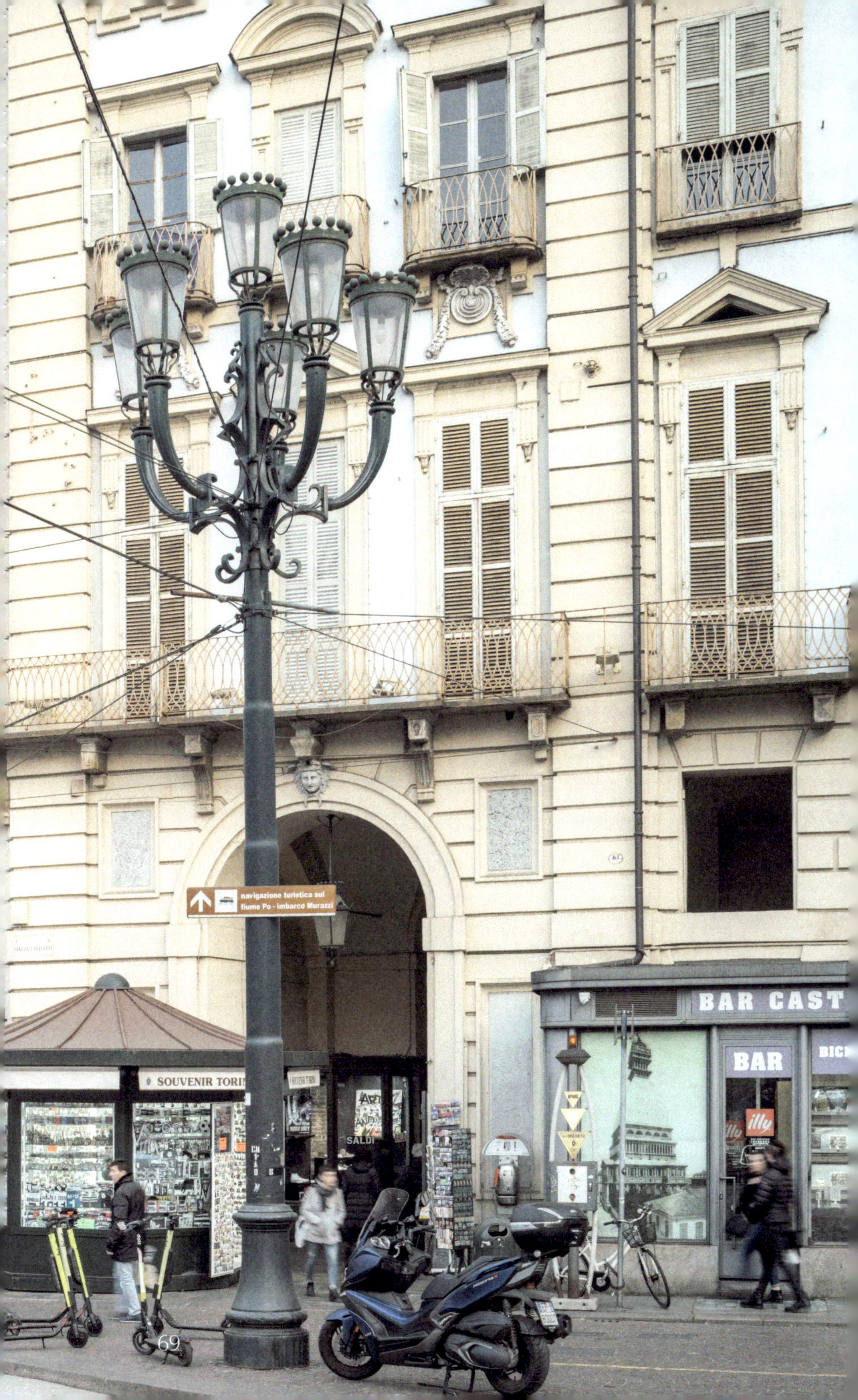
navigazione turistica sul
fiume Po - imbarco Murazzi
SOUVENIR TORIN
SALDI
BAR CAST
BAR
illy

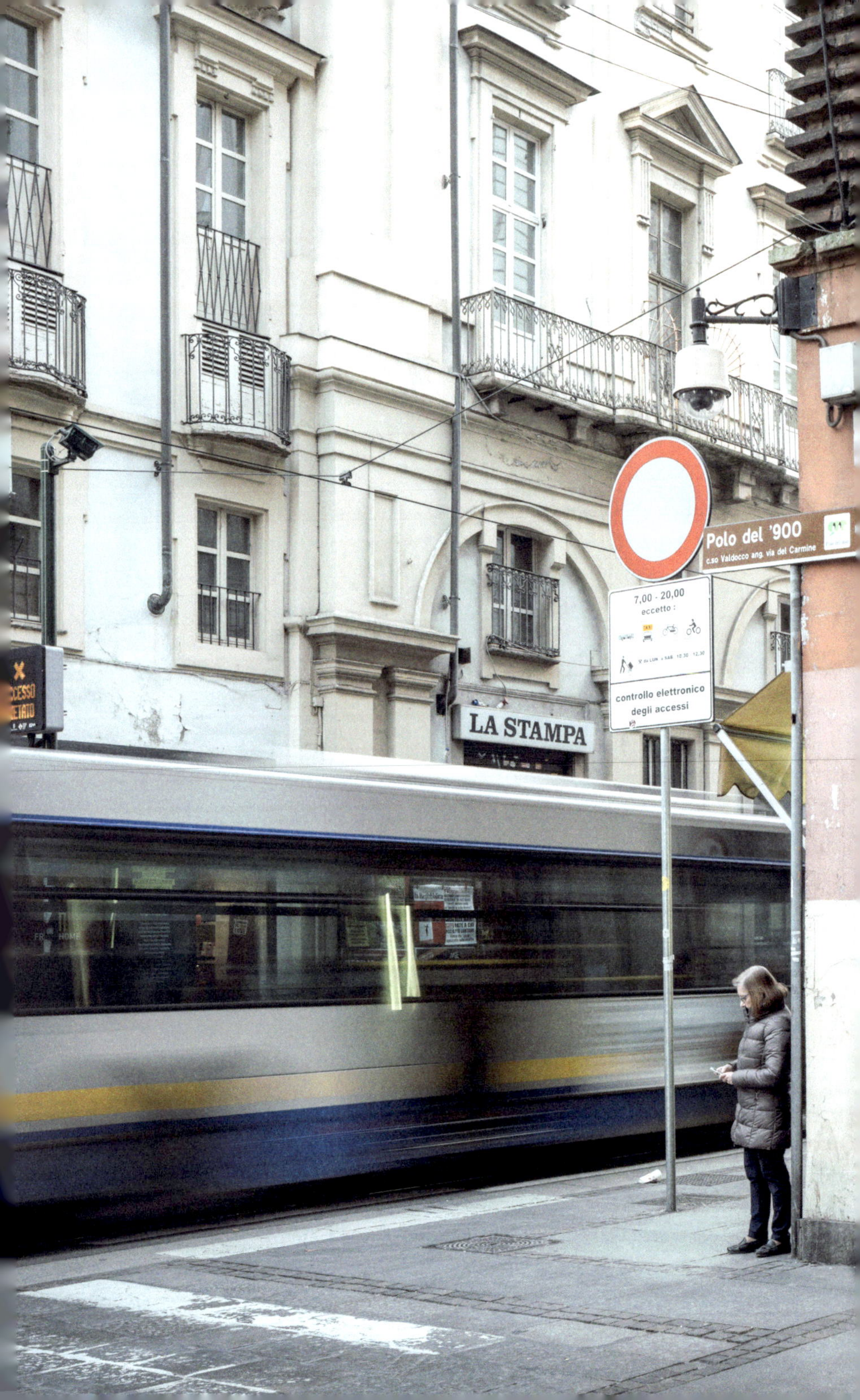
Polo del '900
c.so Valdocco ang. via del Carmine
7,00 - 20,00
eccetto :
controllo elettronico
degli accessi
LA STAMPA

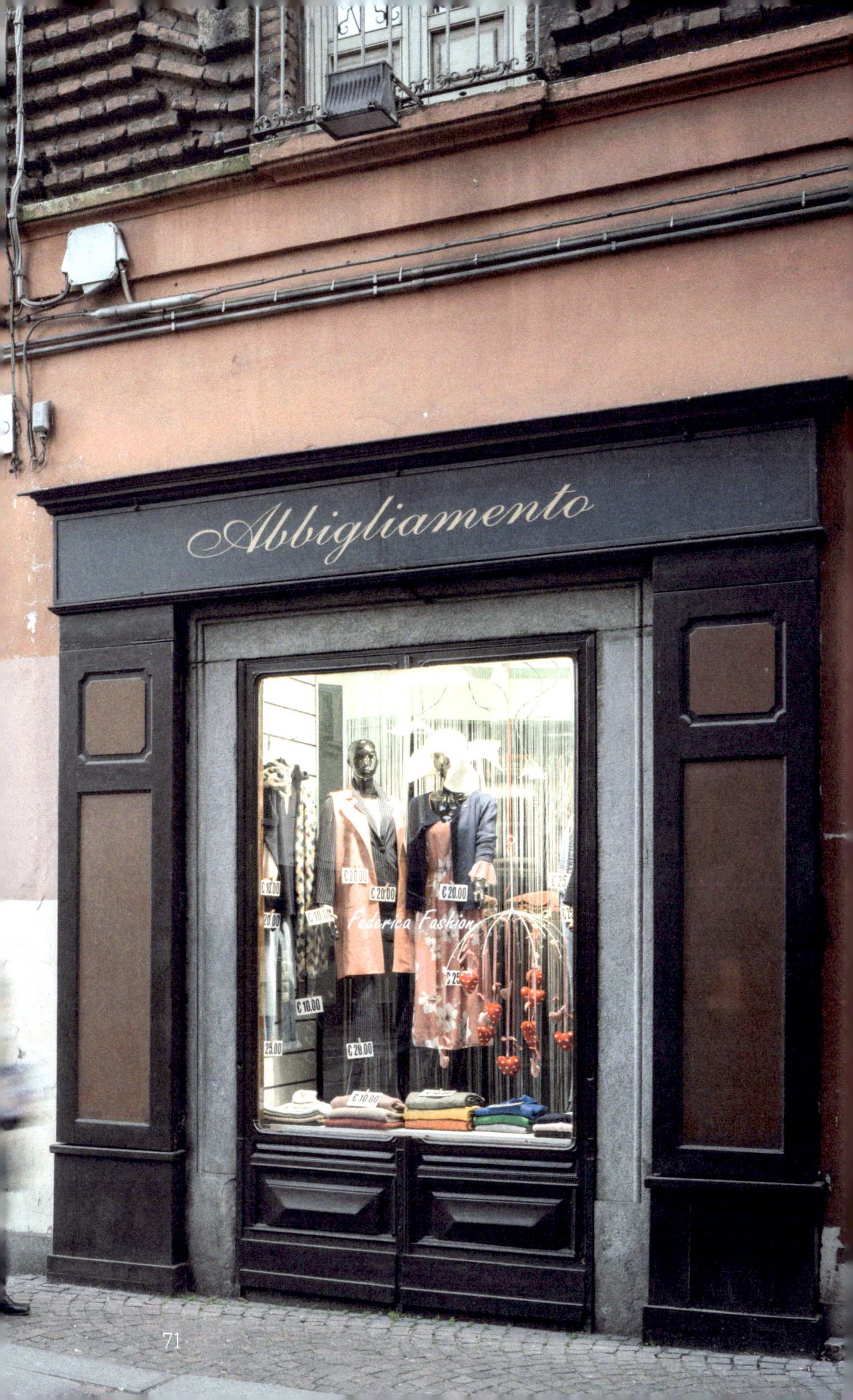
Abbigliamento
Federica Fashion

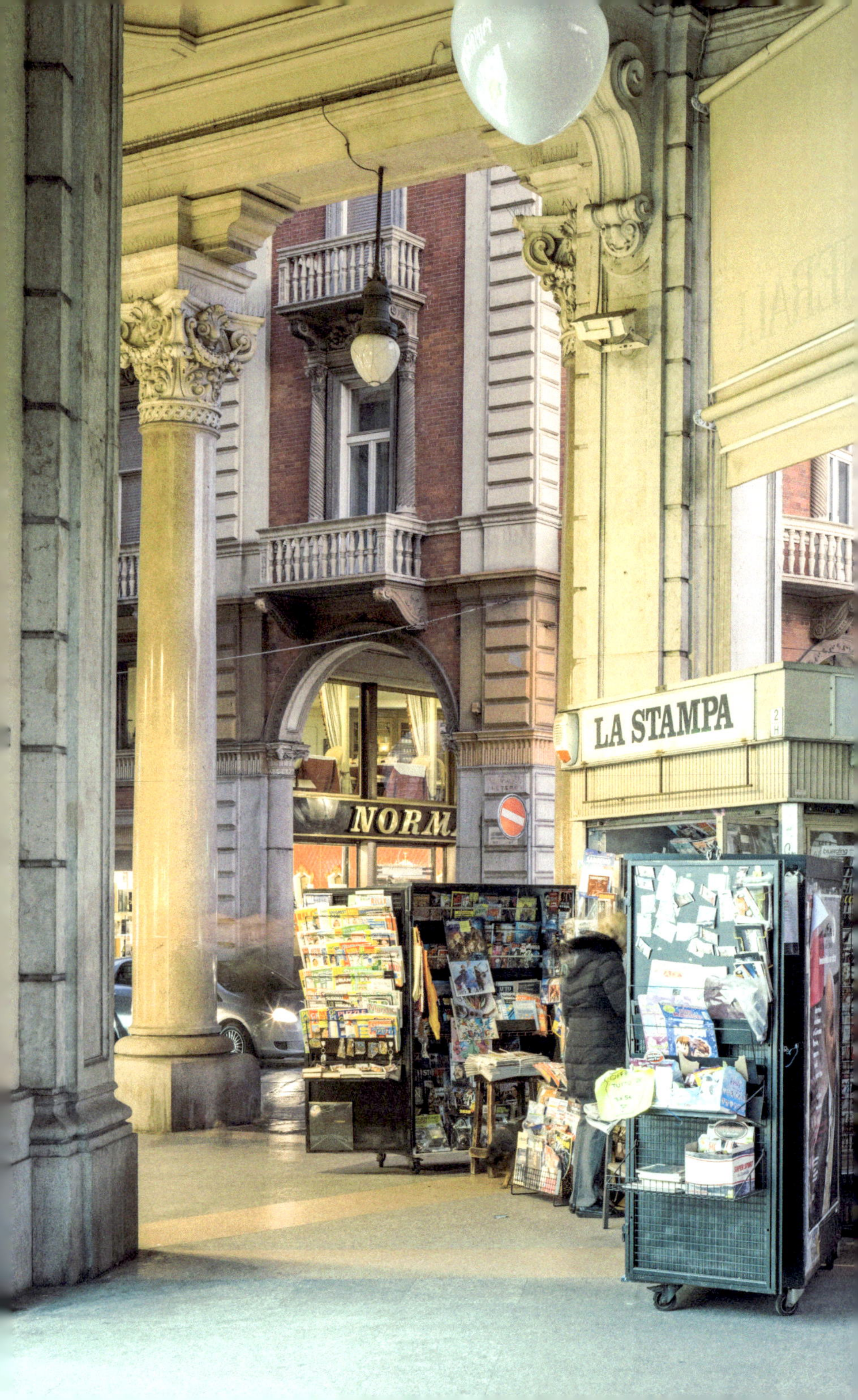
LA STAMPA
NORMA

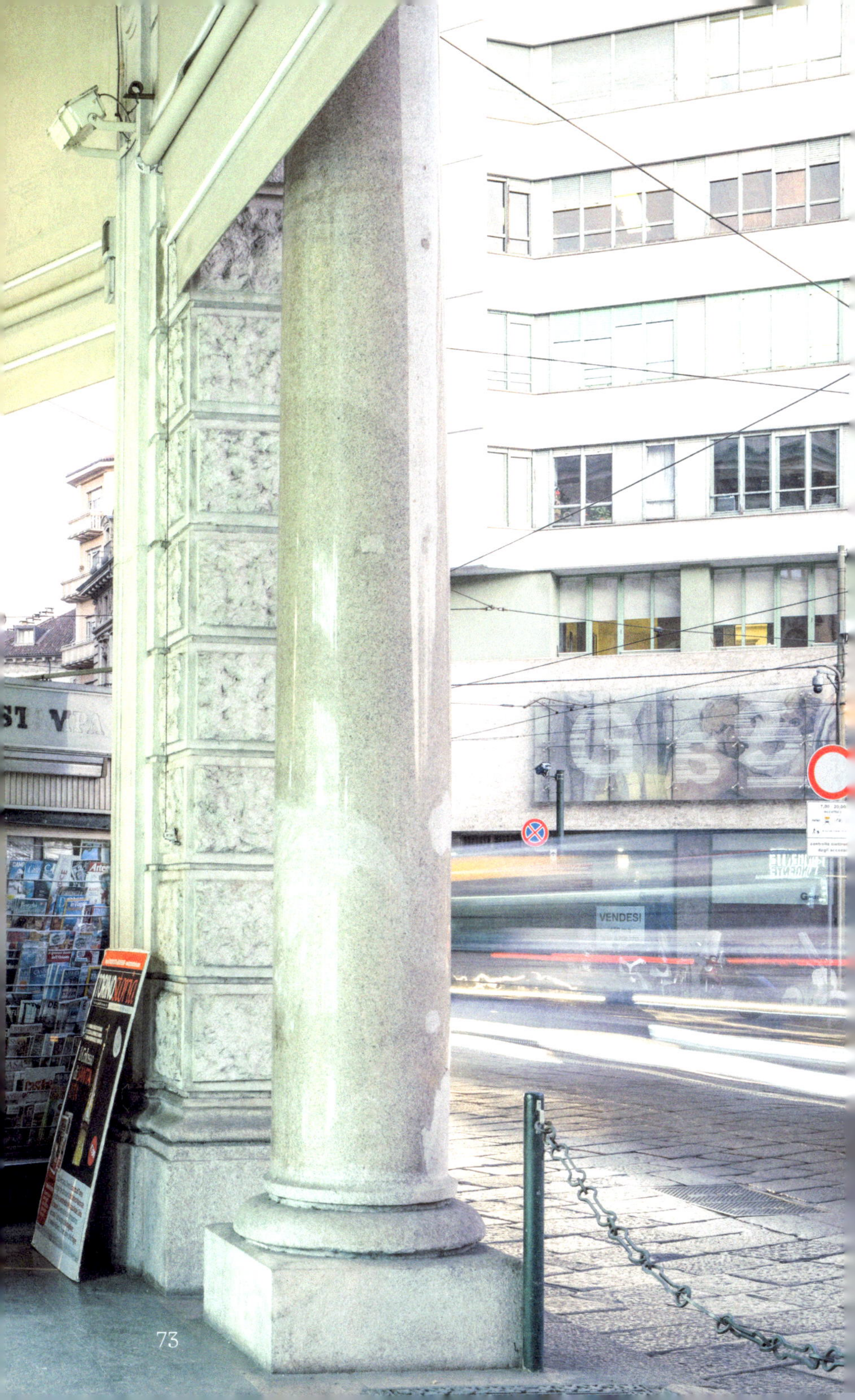
VENDESI

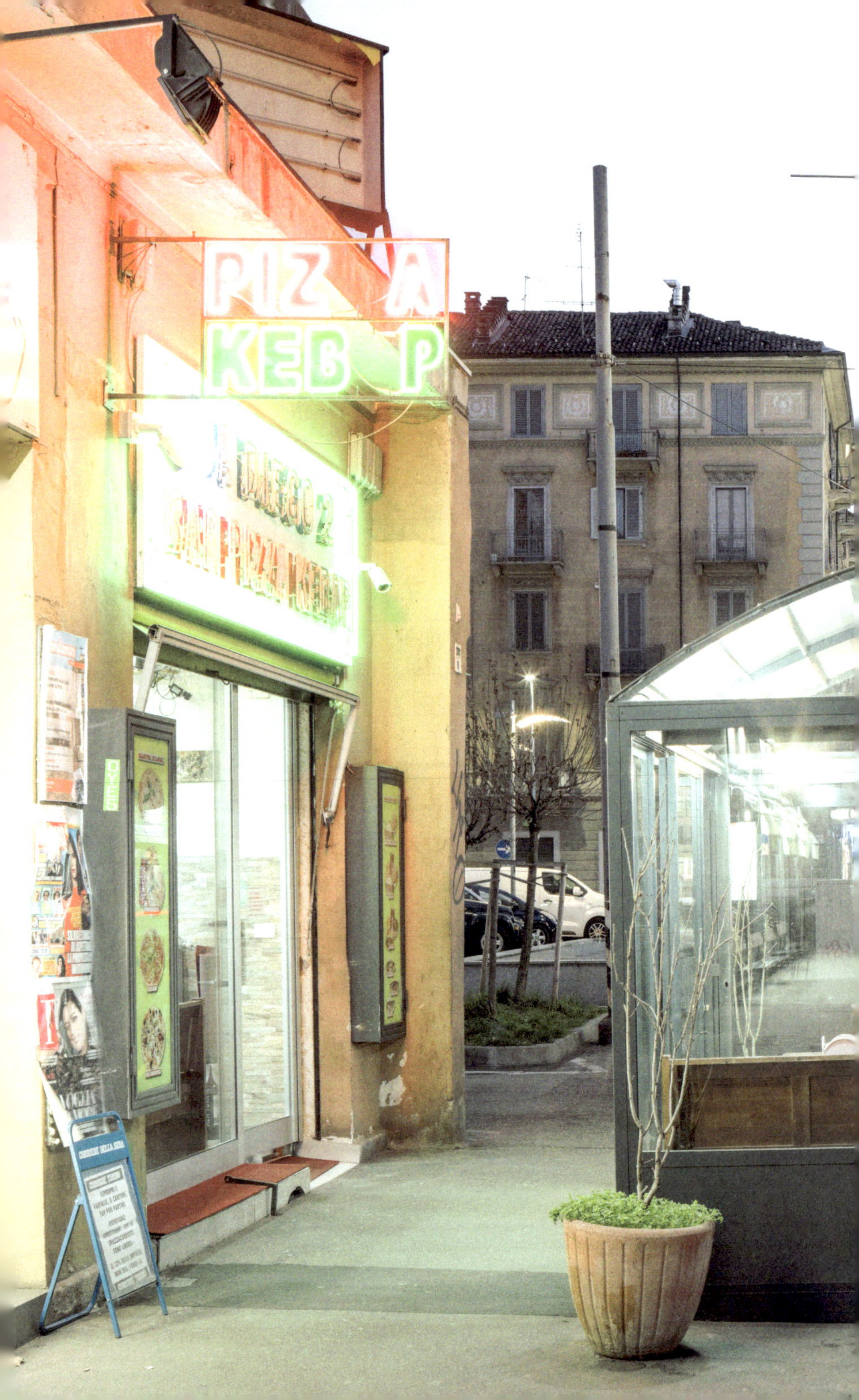
PIZ A
KEB P

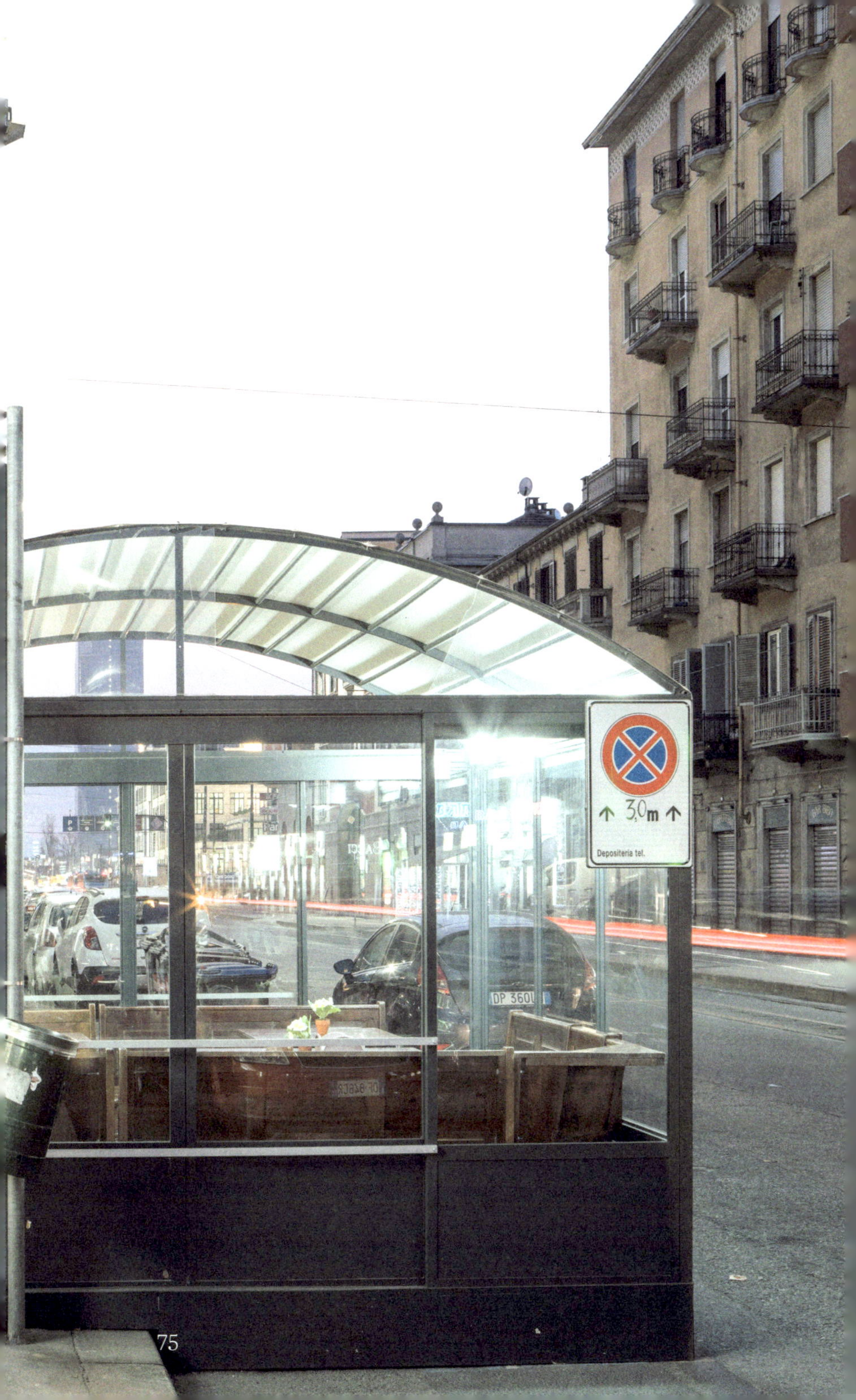
3,0m
Depositeria tel.

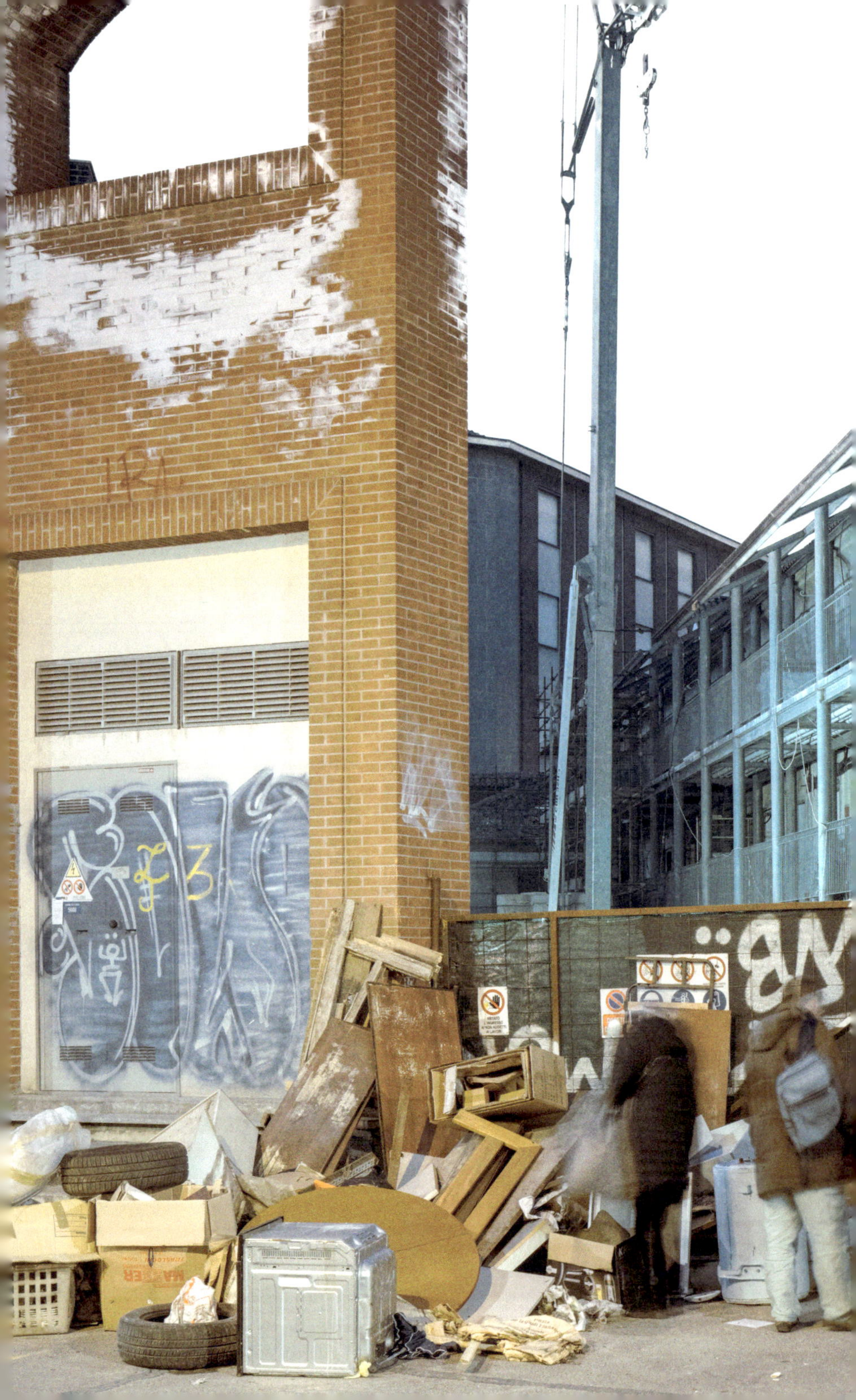

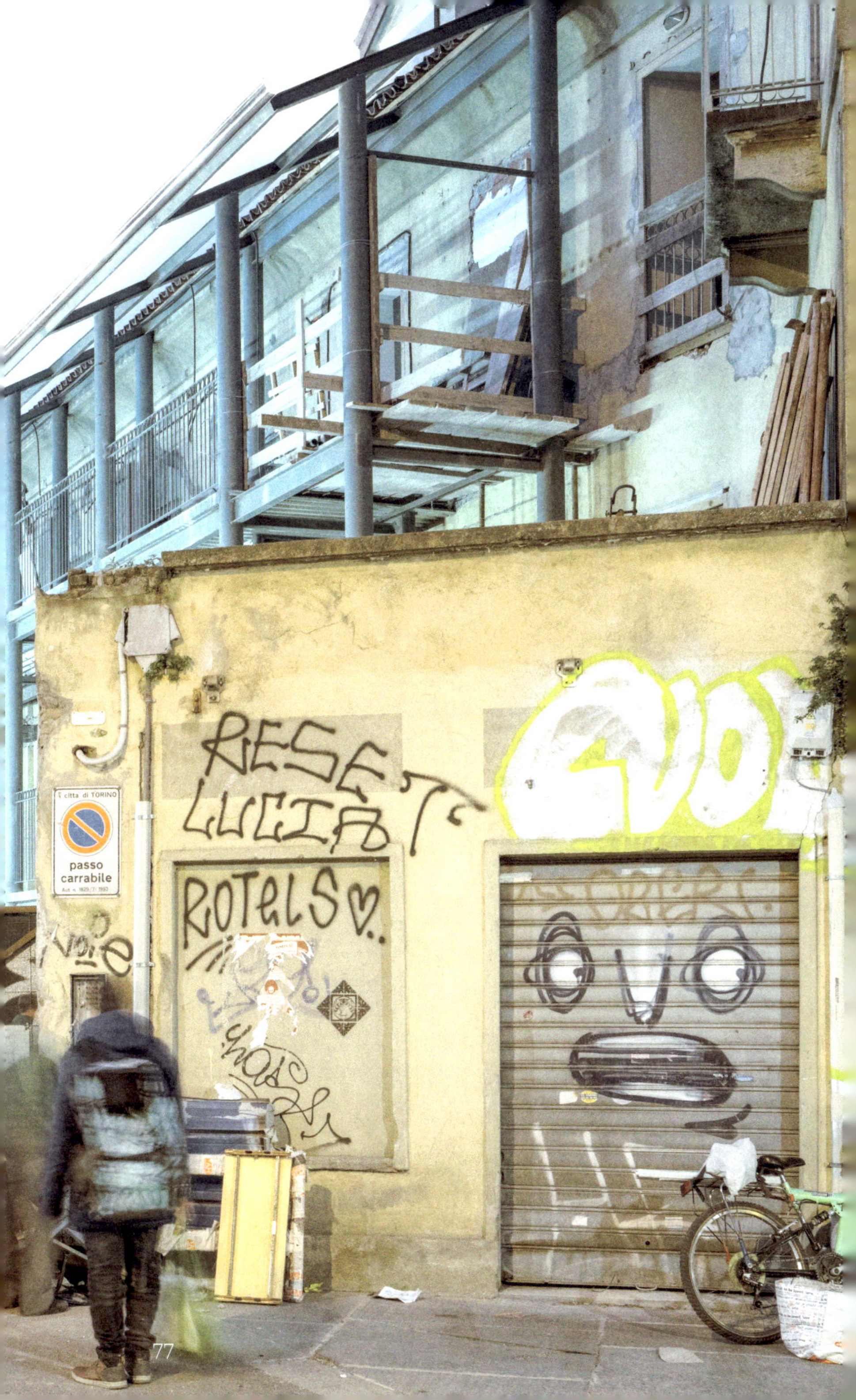
città di TORINO
passo
carrabile

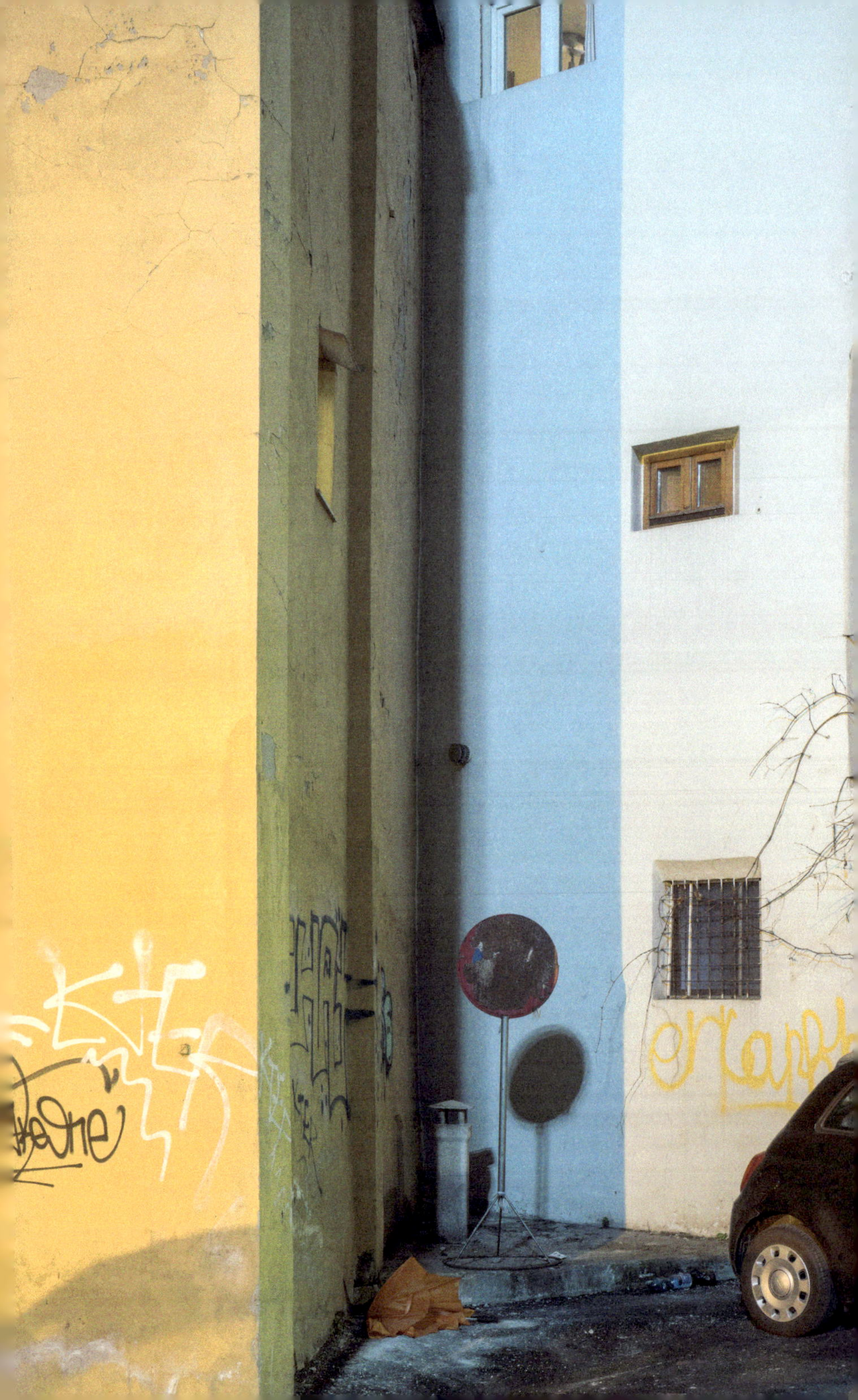

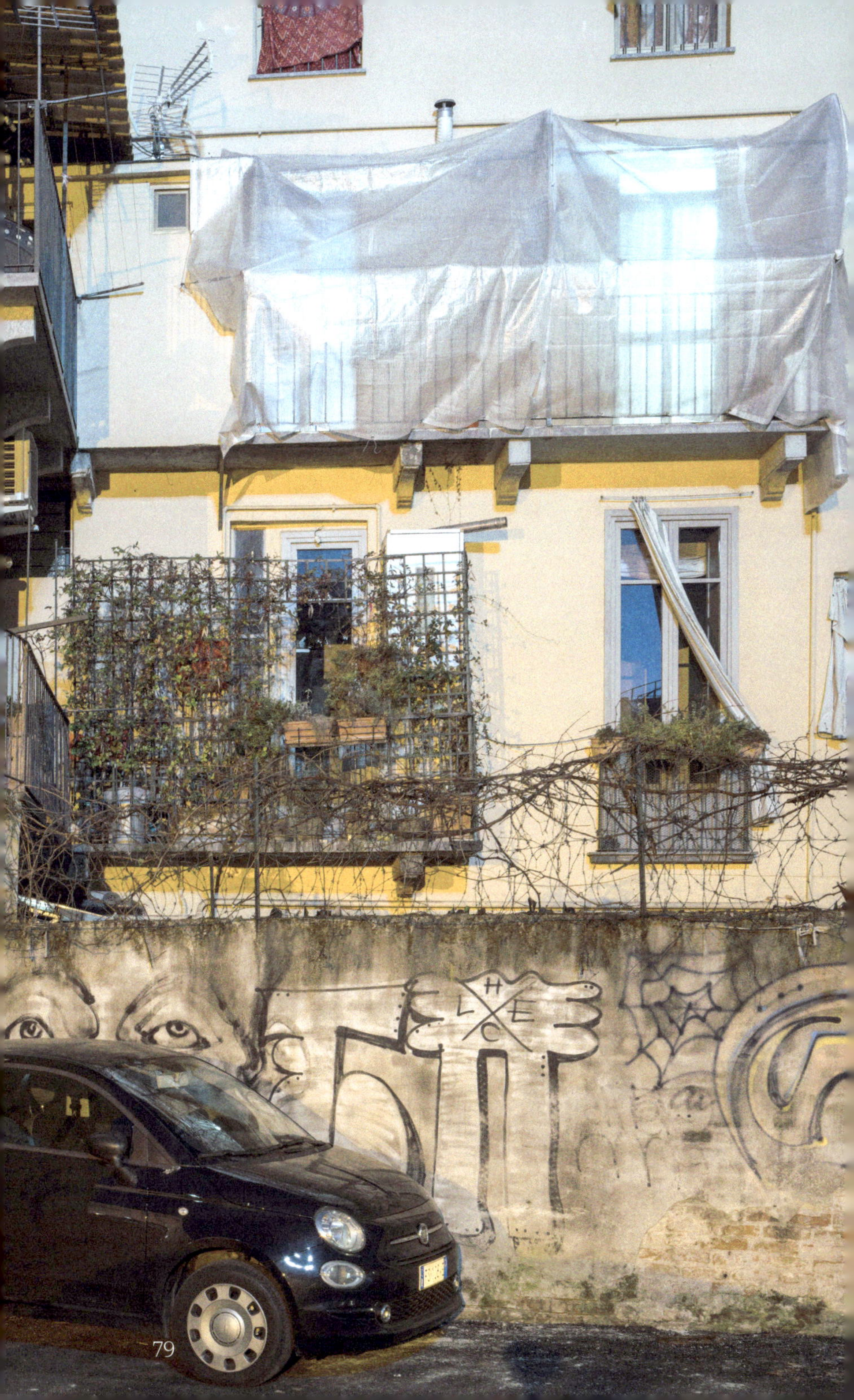
H
L E
C

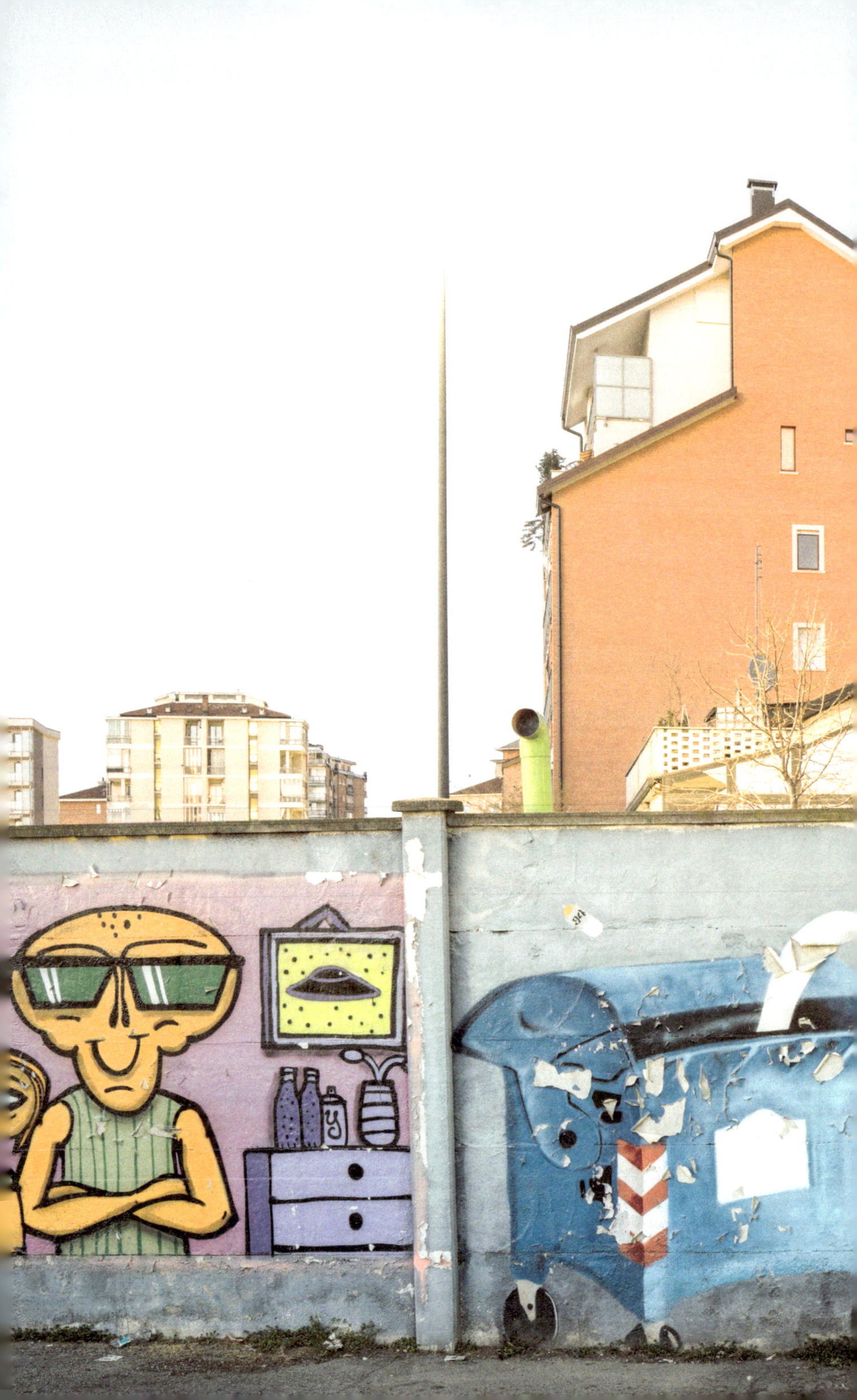

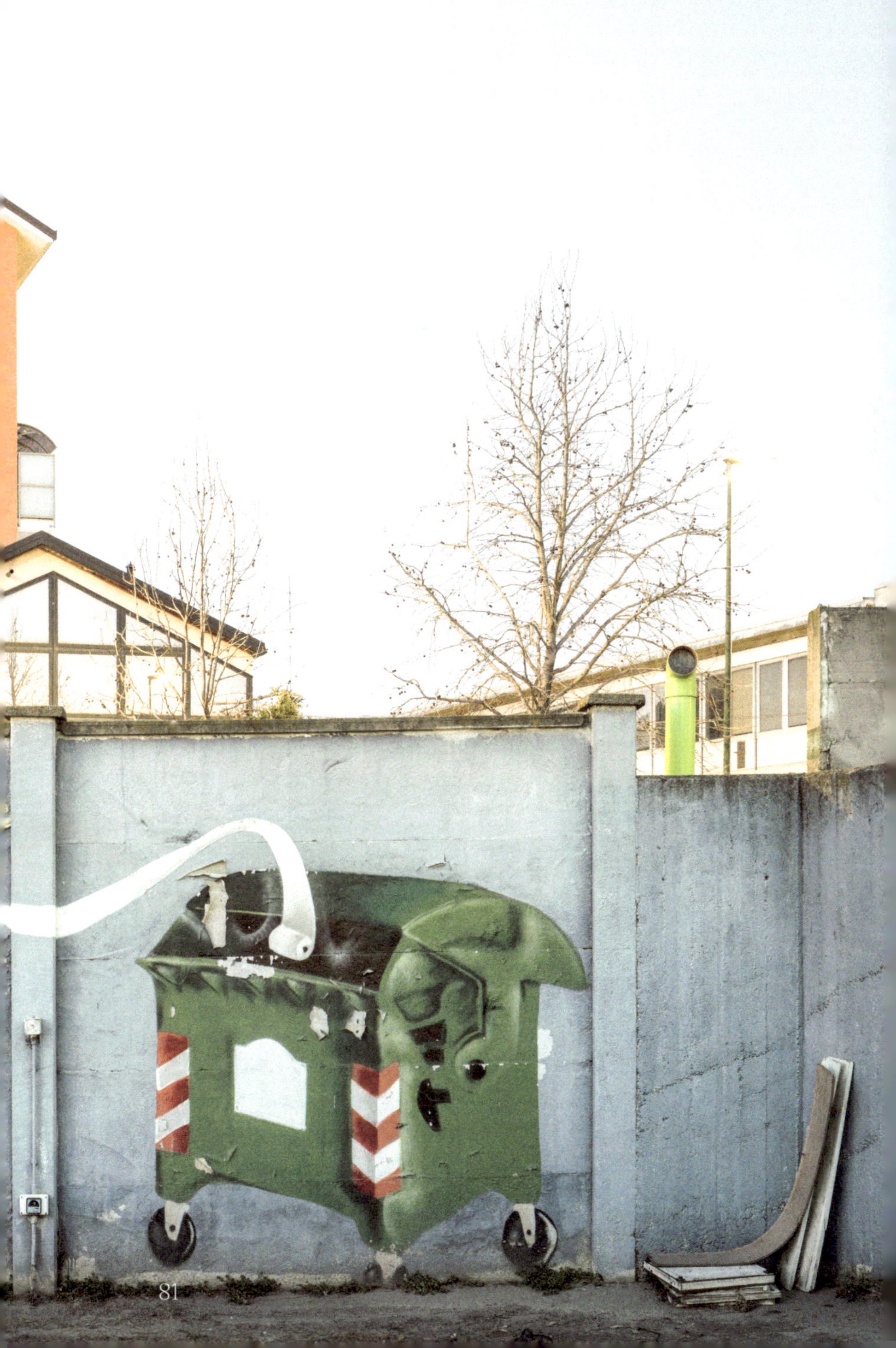

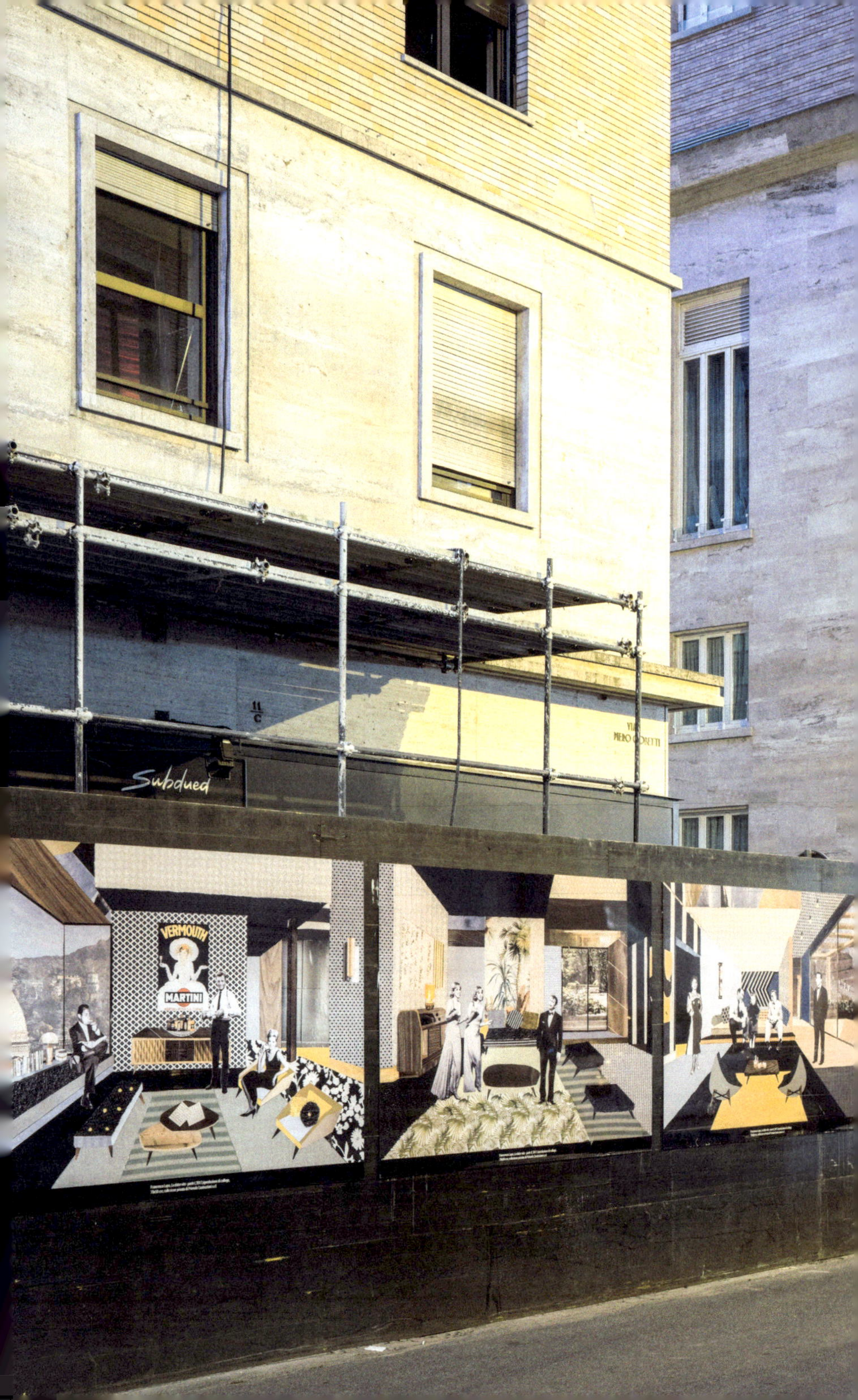
11
C
VIA
PIERO
Subdued
VERMOUTH
MARTINI

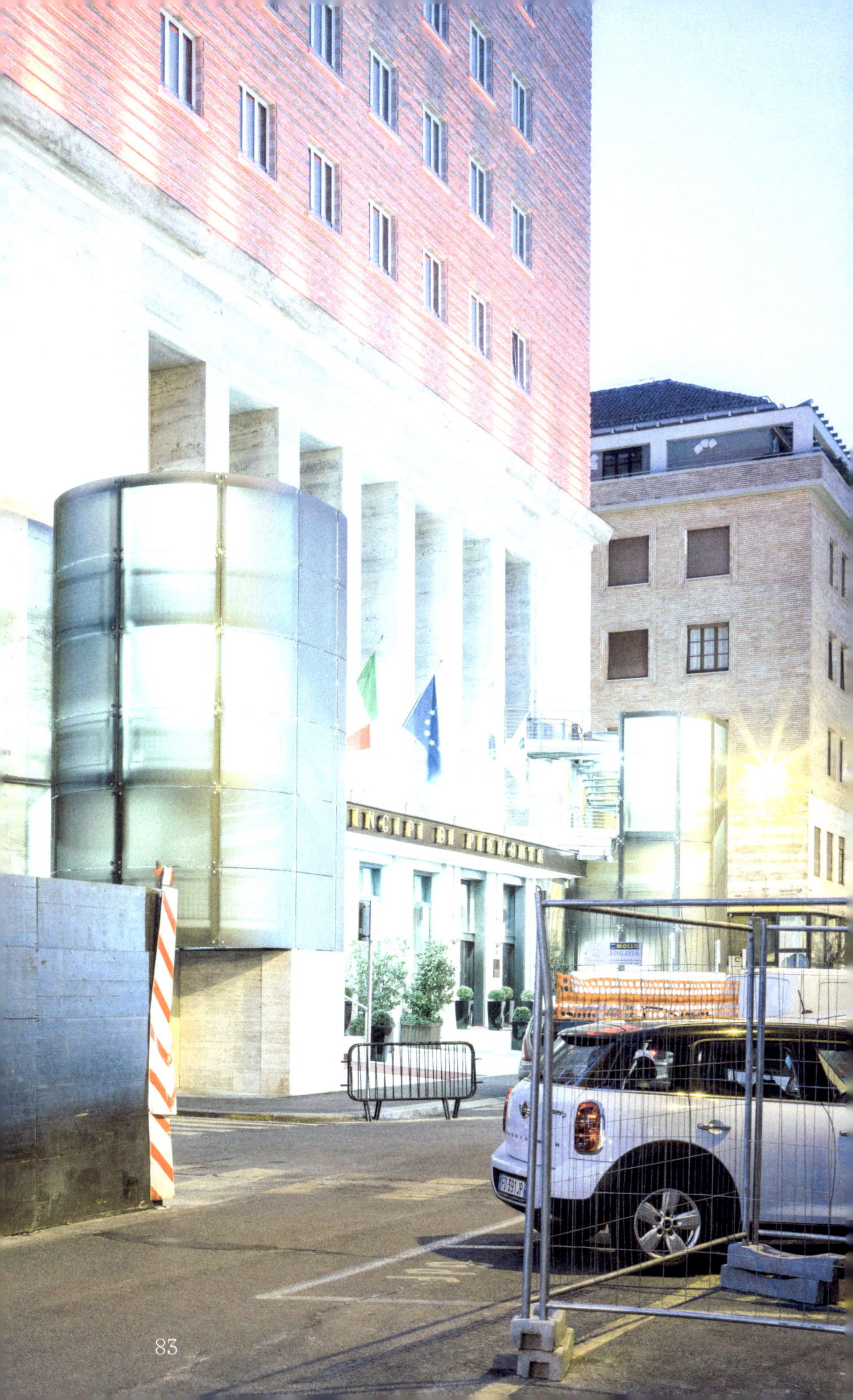
INCIPI DI PIEMONTE
MOLLO
EDILIZIA

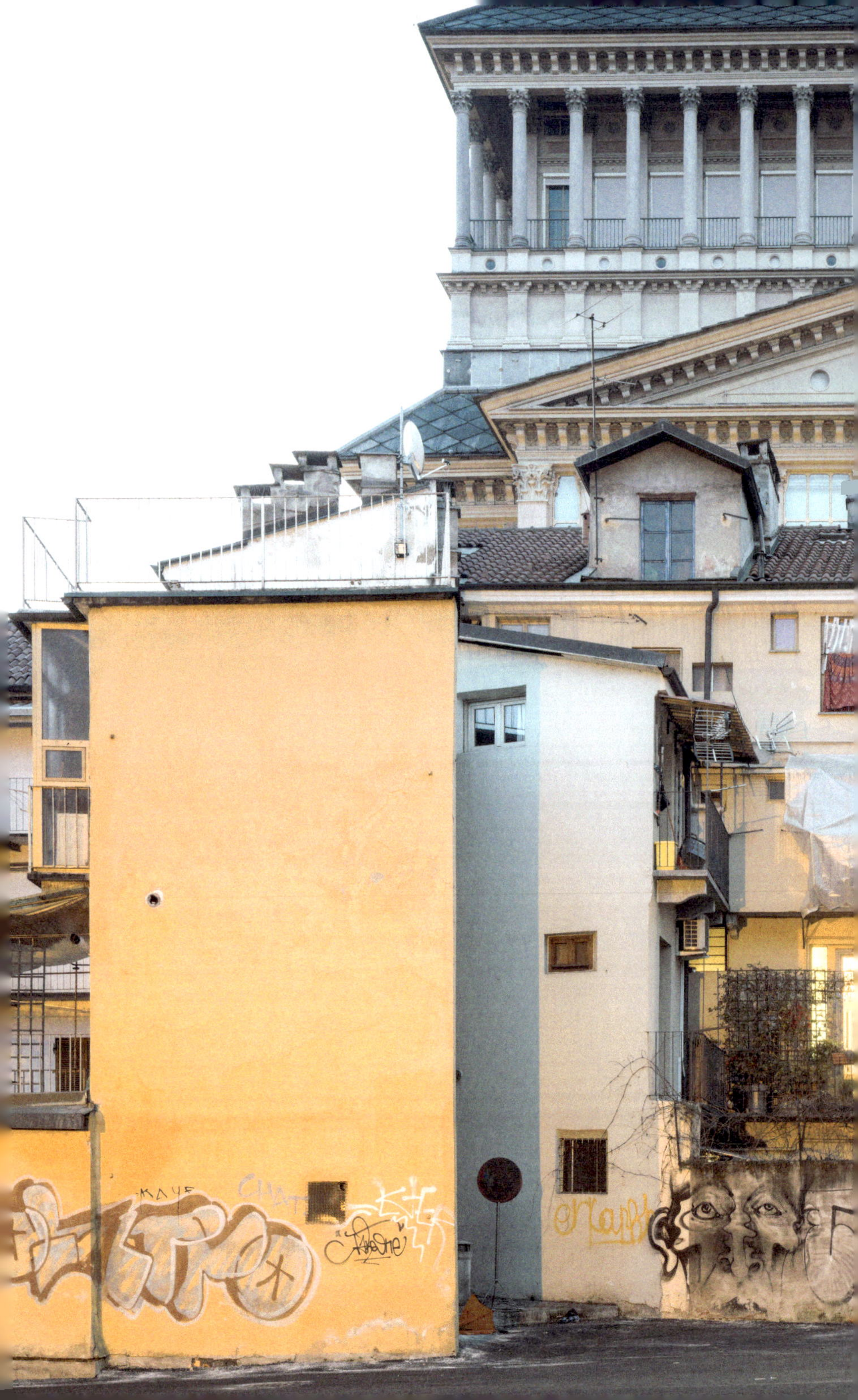

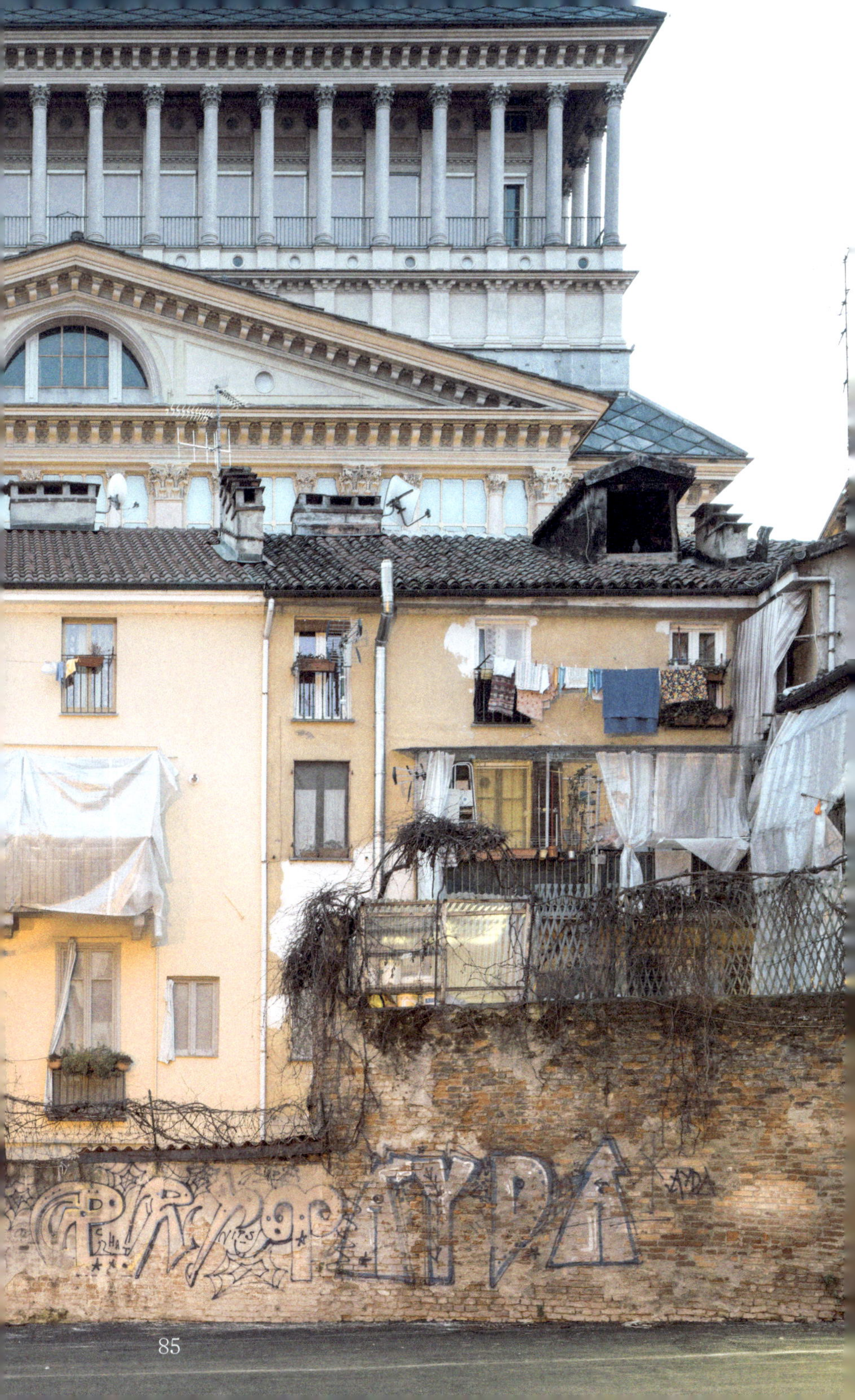

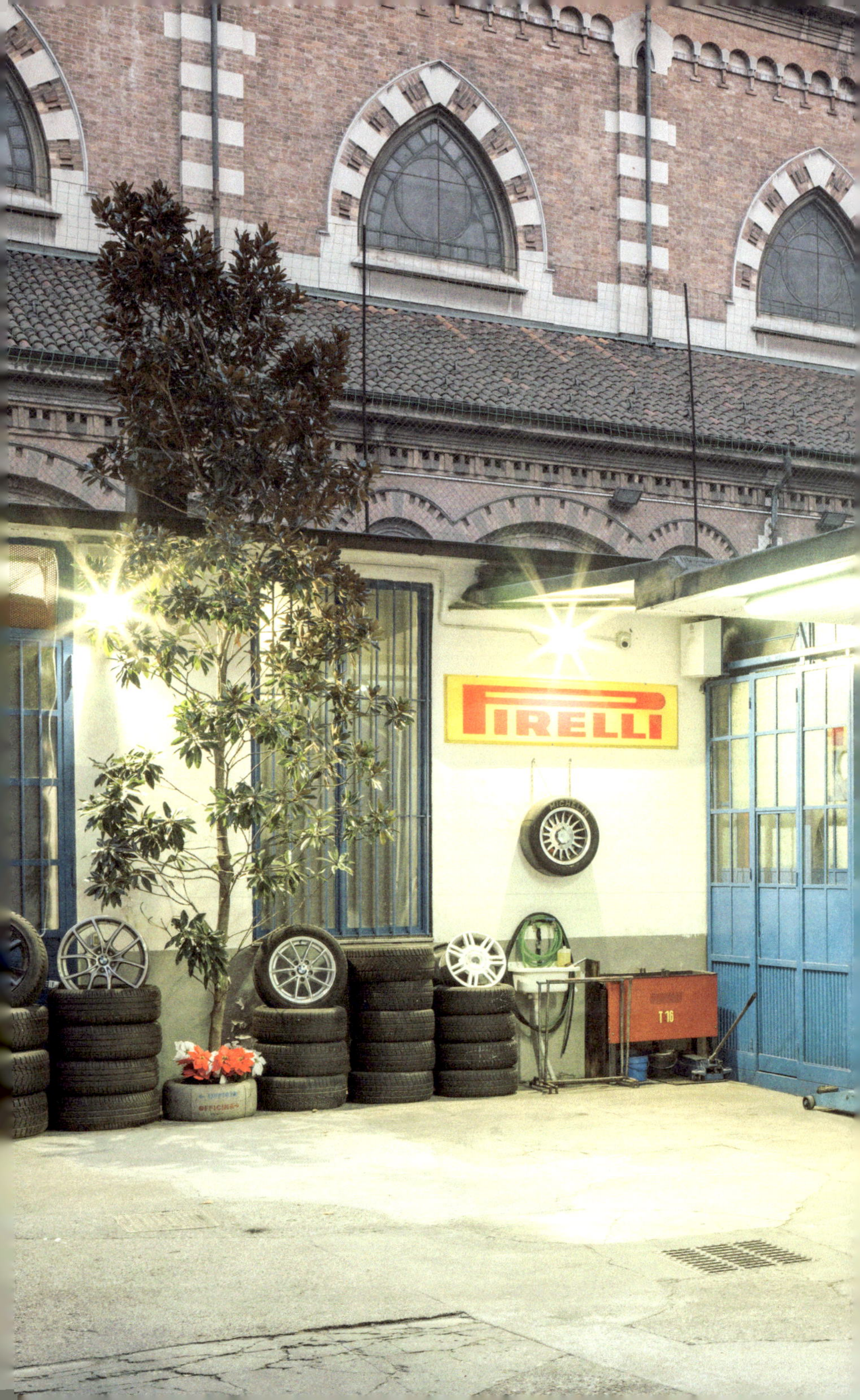
PIRELLI
T 16

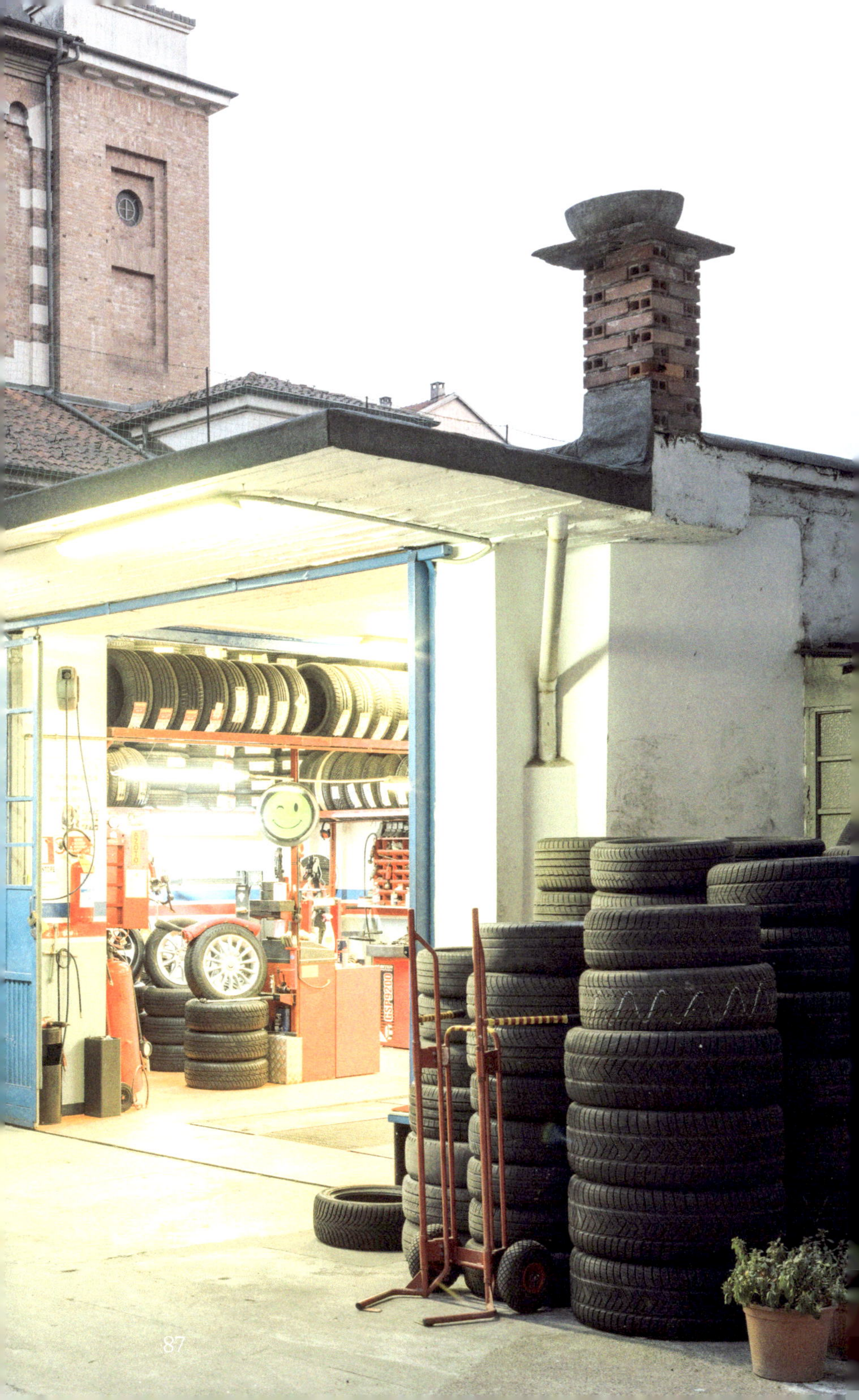

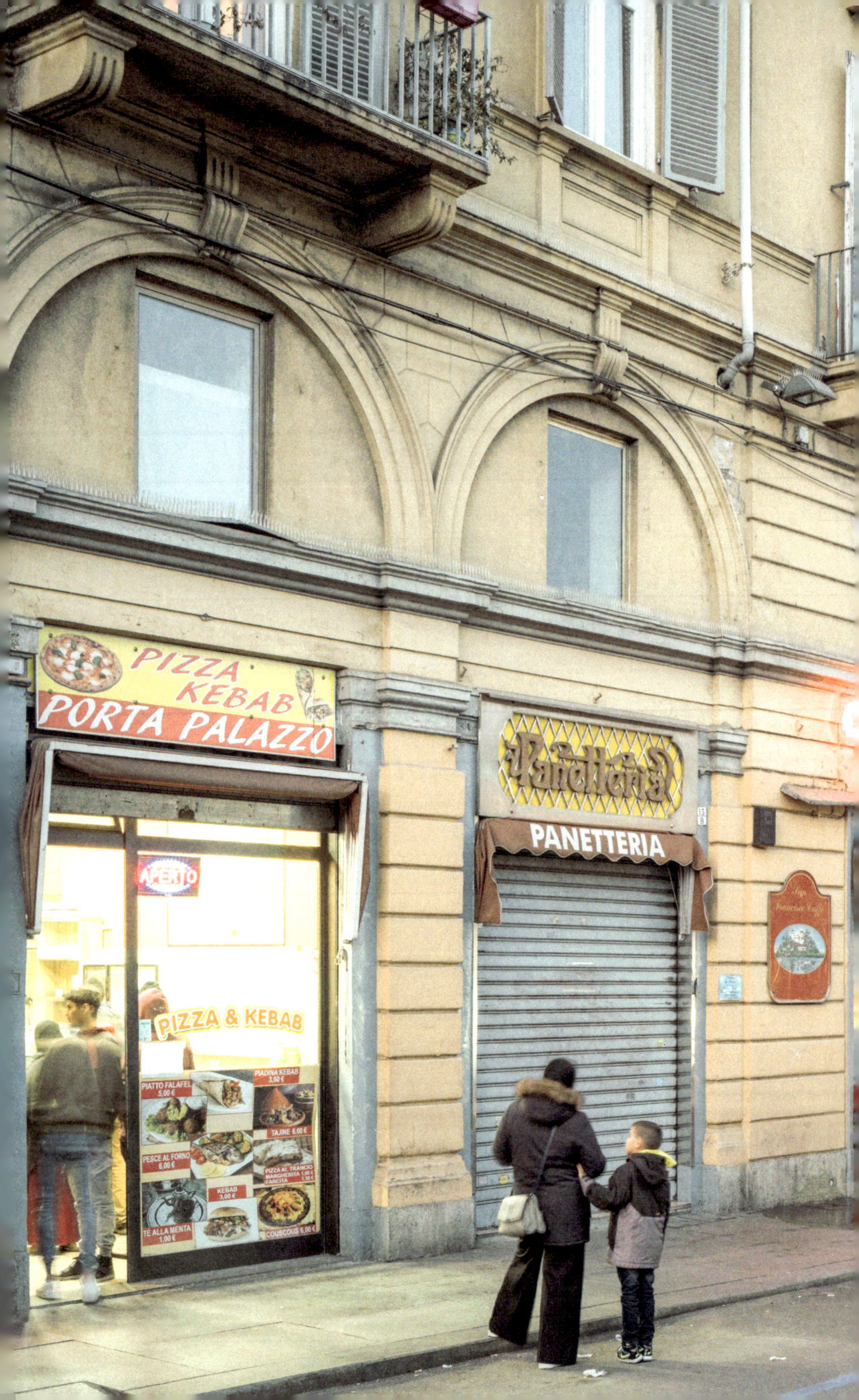
PIZZA
KEBAB
PORTA PALAZZO
APERTO
PIZZA & KEBAB
PIATTO FALAFEL
5,00 €
PIADINA KEBAB
3,50 €
TAJINE 6,00 €
PESCE AL FORNO
6,00 €
KEBAB
3,00 €
TE ALLA MENTA
1,00 €
COUSCOUS 5,00 €
Panetteria
PANETTERIA

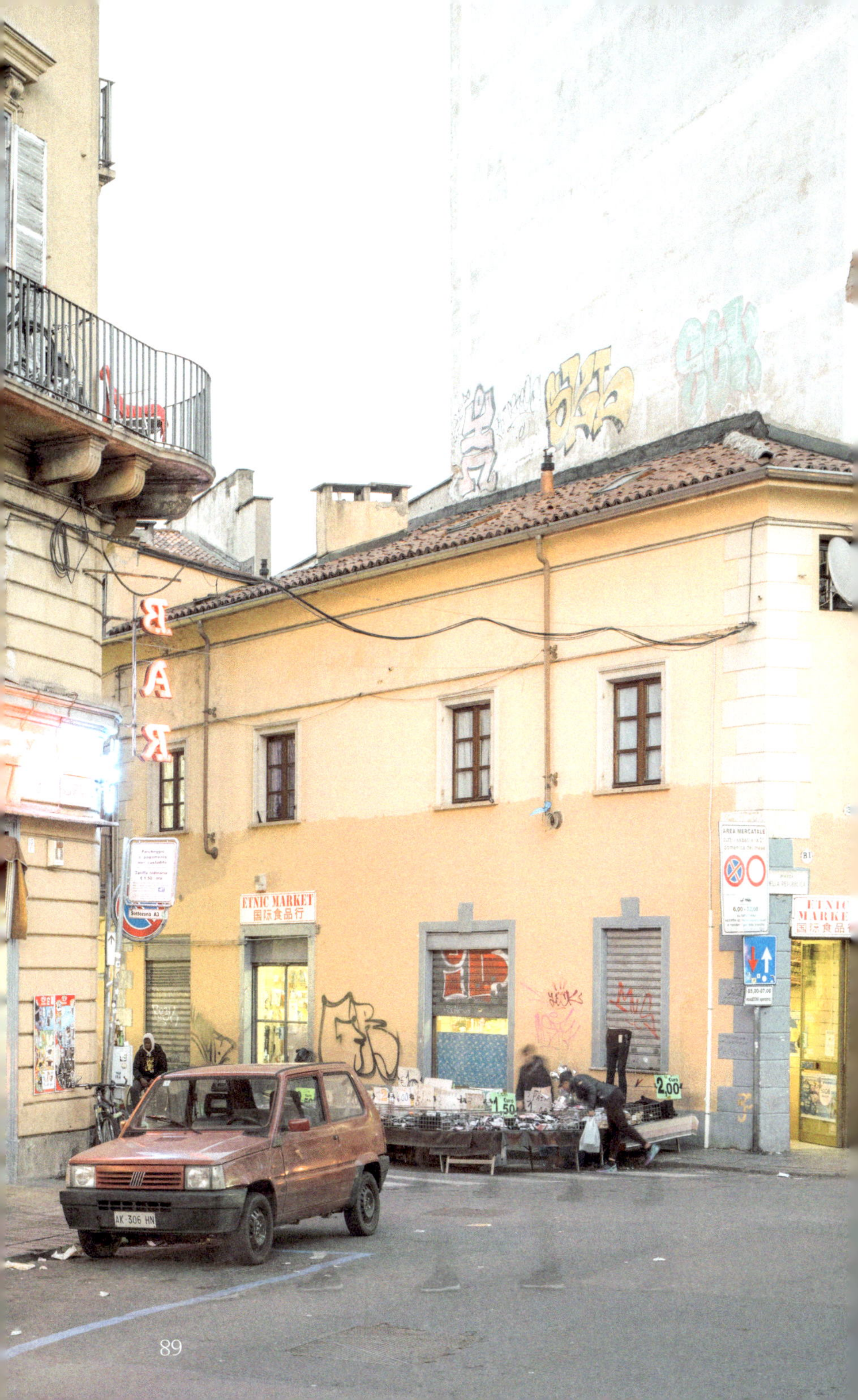
BAR
ETNIC MARKET
国际食品行
AREA MERCATALE
1,50
2,00
AK 306 HN

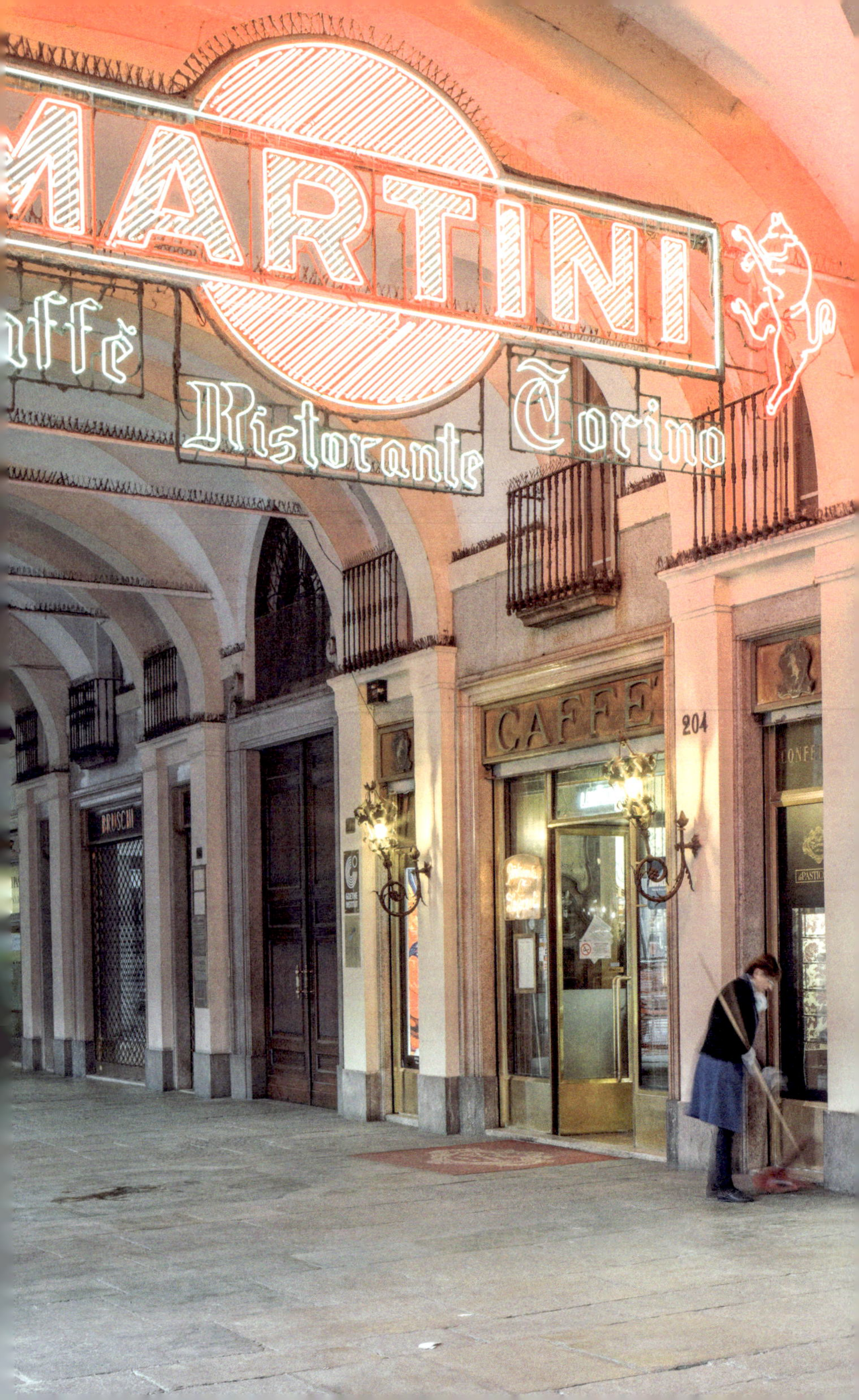
MARTINI
Ristorante
Torino
CAFFE
204

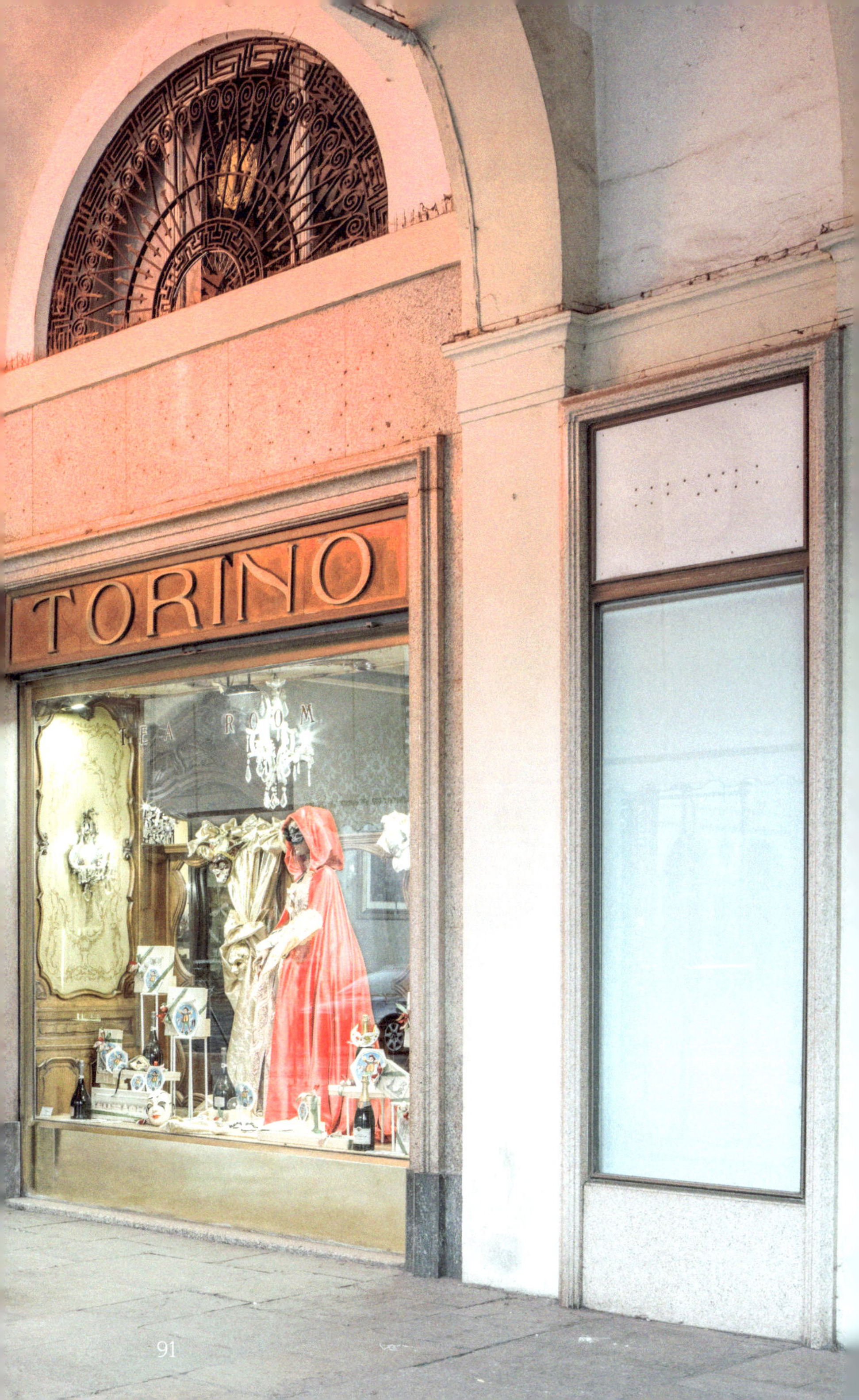
TORINO
TEA ROOM

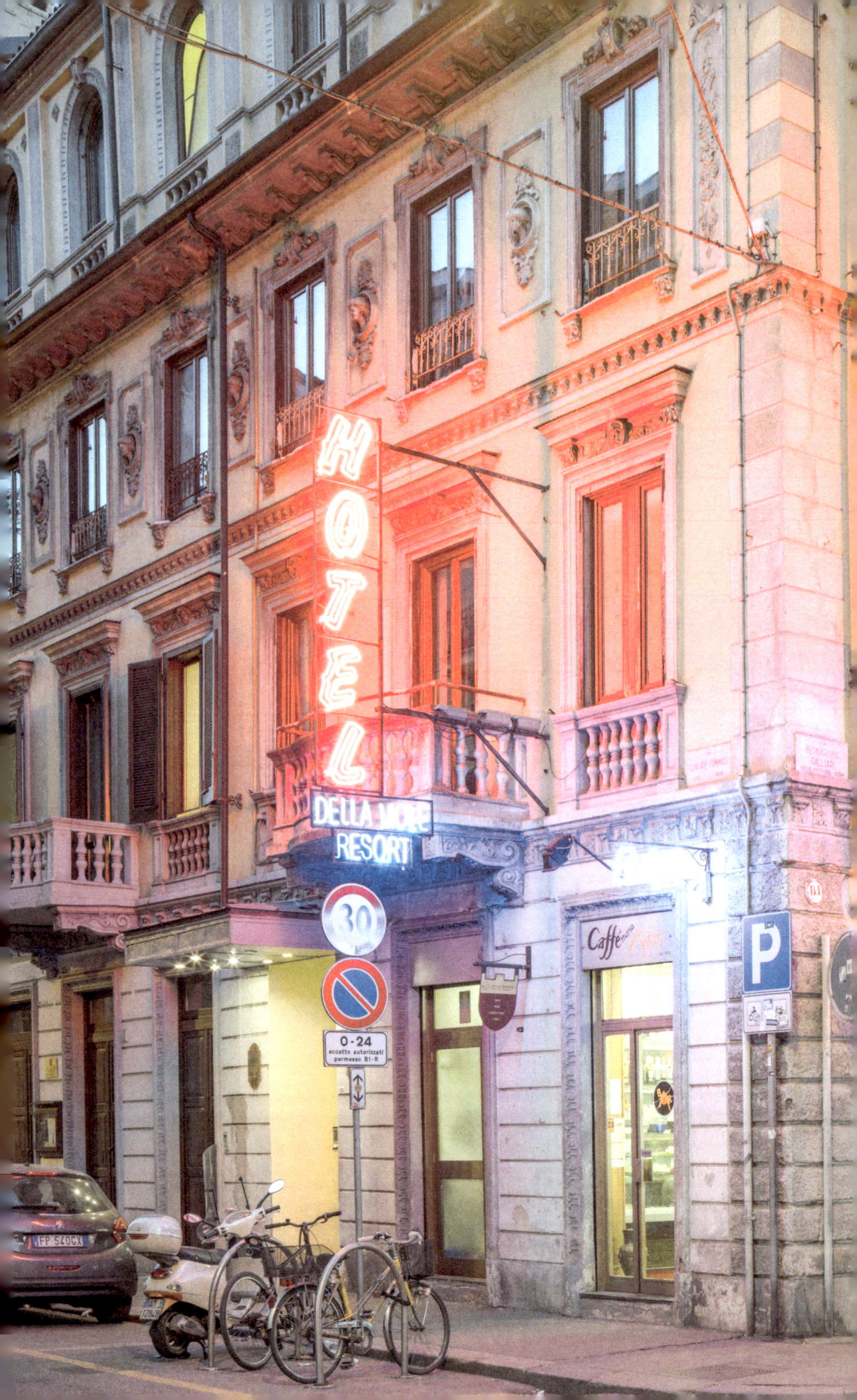
HOTEL
DELLA
RESORT
30
0-24
eccetto autorizzati
permesso B1-R
Caffè
P

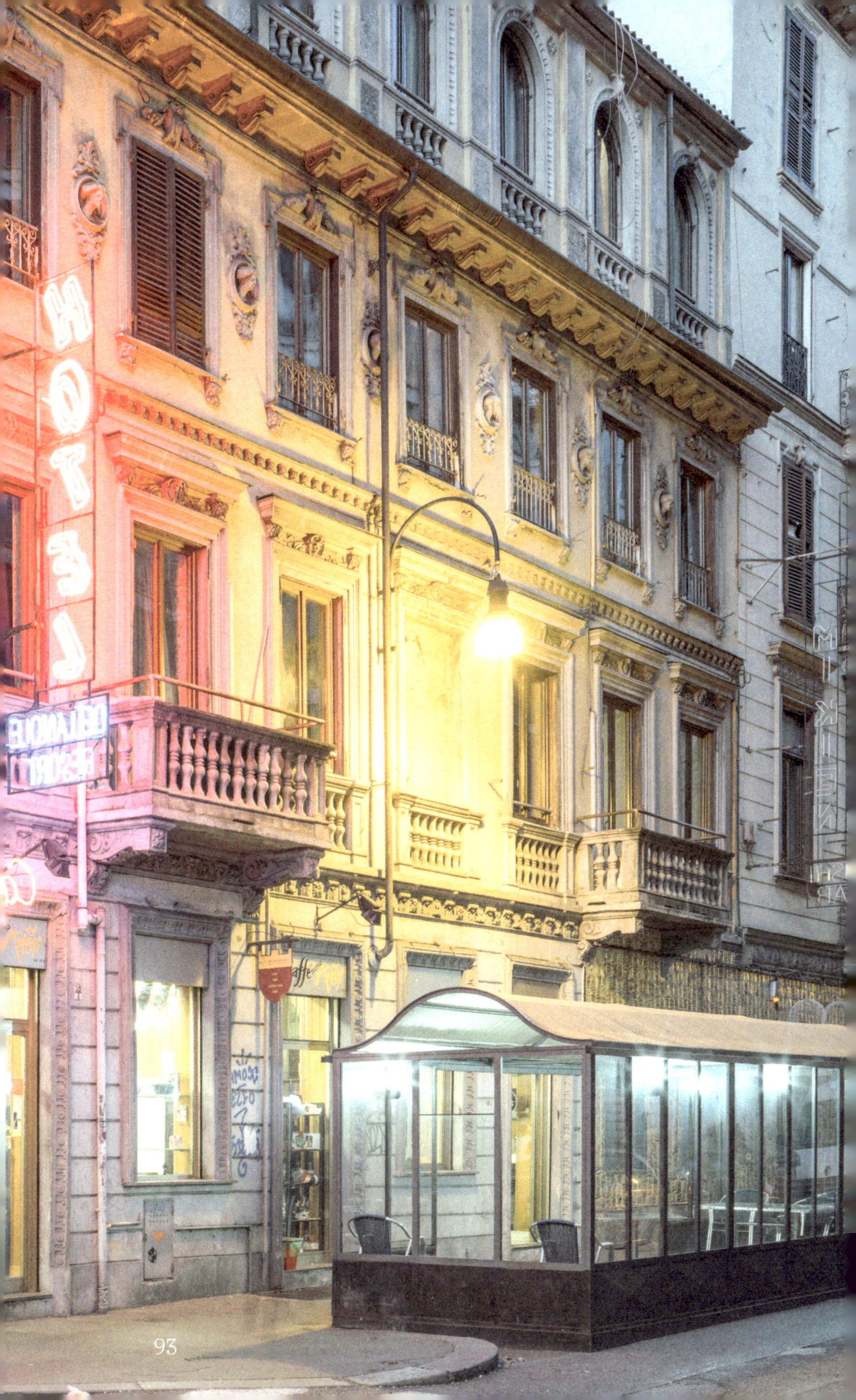

Previous Diaries

Cairo Diary #1
2014
ISBN 978-1-908889-20-1

Athens Diary #2
2015
ISBN 978-1-908889-29-4

Wolfsburg Diary #3
2016
ISBN 978-1-908889-34-8

Taipei Diary #4
2015
ISBN 978-1-908889-30-0

Kochi Diary #5
2018
ISBN 978-1-908889-44-7

Beirut Diary #6
2018
ISBN 978-1-908889-40-9

Wuhan Diary #7
2018
ISBN 978-1-908889-645

Zurich Diary #8
2019
ISBN 978-1-908889-65-2

Budapest Diary #9
2020
ISBN 978-1-908889-66-9

Osaka Diary #10
2020
ISBN 978-1-908889-56-0

Dhaka Diary #11
2021
ISBN 978-1-908889-86-7

Yangon Diary #12
2021
ISBN 978-1-908889-87-4

Minsk Diary #13
2021
ISBN 978-1-908889-88-1

Belfast Diary #14
2021
ISBN 978-1-908889-89-8

Linz Diary #15
2021
ISBN 978-1-908889-90-4

The previous diaries have been published by *thevelvetcell.com* and are available through the website.

George Town Diary #16
2022
ISBN 978-3-96070-090-6

Unna Diary #17
2022
ISBN 978-3-96070-089-0

Sarajevo Diary #18
2022
ISBN 978-3-96070-088-3

Bangkok Diary #19
2022
ISBN 978-3-96070-087-6

Vilnius Diary #20
2024
ISBN 978-3-96070-105-7

Turin Diary #21
2024
ISBN 978-3-96070-103-3

Wilson Diary #22
2024
ISBN 978-3-96070-106-4

London Diary #23
2024
ISBN 978-3-96070-104-0

Turin Diary
Peter Bialobrzeski

Published by
Hartmann Books
Liststraße 28/1
70180 Stuttgart
hartmann-books.com

Photographs
Peter Bialobrzeski
bialobrzeski.net

Graphic Design and Typesetting
Sarah Fricke, Distaff Studio

Copyediting
Tas Skorupa, New York

Printing and Binding
DZA Druckerei zu Altenburg

Paper
Pergraphica Natural Rough

Typefaces
ABC Diatype, GT Alpina

First Edition, 2024
500 copies

ISBN
978-3-96070-103-3

For Eanna

This project was realized in
collaboration with *Jest*, Turin